Parenting in the Real World.

THE REBOOT OF PARENTING.

OLIVIA BLACK

PARENTING IN THE REAL WORLD:
The Reboot of Parenting.
©2016 Olivia Black

Published by Brevard Marketing LLC
CreateSpace Independent Publishing Platform

ISBN-13: 978-1522781509
ISBN-10: 1522781501

table of contents

forward by reverend jake mcgrew

What is written on the following pages may, at first, appear to be painfully sarcastic. Truth usually hurts. I may never admit this professionally or socially, but no matter how you look at it, very few men voluntarily become a father. Typically, he's in her pants for one reason and one reason only. And, although she'll never admit it, I'd wager that quite a few mothers became mothers as a method to attain a certain lifestyle.

Some unseen, unknown, all-knowing being, or force, or whatever of the more than 3,000 deities you believe in apparently thinks it's comical to give you the biological equipment for the ultimate human pleasure, and punish you with a ball and chain that will stand in the way of you getting any more of that physical pleasure for the next twenty years. Supposedly, He's smart enough to create life, a functional planet, and a universe. But He purposely forgets to leave a *manual?* Look, I'm a man of the cloth, and even I think that's ridiculous. As a two-time father with stepchildren, Olivia Black's sarcasm is well deserved.

According to the unwritten manual we civilized humans have devised over the past 40,000 years, parenting is viewed as one of those normal life events all of us are supposed to experience. You grow up, you get married, you land a job you may despise, and then you have children. Eventually, your kids grow up, you get old, and return to the dirt from which you came. That's the master plan. Many of us believe this entire world is a temporary pass-through, or perhaps a test, for a glorious afterlife. In my humble upbringing, I was raised to think that I was meant to be poor, parenting was a punishment for something I couldn't possibly comprehend, and that's why so many folks were alcoholics. Sorry to cast such a negative dispersion on parenting, but that's how modern society tends to view it.

Long story short, after about three decades of having sex, I ended up with a son that's definitely mine, and a grown daughter whose mother has told me on several occasions she may not actually be my daughter. I think I'm a pretty good father, considering I didn't have much to go on.

If you still have half a brain that hasn't been overrun with fluoride or microwave poisoning, you're probably beginning to get a little nervous. Soon, you too will be asking yourself the same question I ask myself each and every day – "How the hell am I supposed to raise a child in this environment?"

No worries, because Olivia Black has it all figured out. She's one of the brightest people I know. If anyone can guide you through raising a perfect child, it's Olivia. So sit back and throw back a cold one – you're going to need it – and join her on this wildlife adventure called *parenthood*. You're stuck now, so you may as well make the most of it. It's fun. It's confusing. It's thankless. It's rewarding. It sucks. It's wonderful. It's punitive. It's cognizant. It's ridiculous.

Parenting is a bunch of things. The one thing it ain't is *reversible*.

-Reverend Jake McGrew

1: why do people have children?

I must admit, birth is indeed a miracle. Considering the fuzzy math behind a woman's fertility cycle, how long sperm live, and nature's own internal filtering system, a successful pregnancy is little more than a crapshoot. The sheer chemistry, or overall science behind the little we understand about conception, birth, and life in general is frightening. There is so much that can and often does go wrong before, during, and after childbirth. Countless healthy women have suffered through sadness and hopeless dejection with miscarriages.

Being saddled down with a tiny life-sucking parasite milking you dry in every way possible is the single most thankless job to which any of us will ever commit. Once you have a child, I am a staunch believer that it is your responsibility to completely care for your offspring, whether the conception of that child was voluntary or not. Having a kid is like joining the mob – once you're initiated, there ain't no getting out. *Ever.* And your life will never be the same. Expect everything – your friends, your hobbies, your spare time, and your financial status – to change drastically. That's just the way it goes.

If you're in this parenting situation for the first time, get ready for an adventure like no other. Think of it like going to school, but with no teacher, no textbook, and no do-overs. There is no official guide that will show you how to be a good parent. Ironically, you can learn how to pick up women, steal a car, hack a computer, or even build a meth lab on YouTube, but you won't find anything worthwhile pertaining to parenting secrets. You've got professional yentas with PhDs and pseudo-celebrity wahoos running around pretending to be experts in child-rearing. Granted, some are very intelligent people. And then there's Tan Mom.

Look, I'm sure you've been inundated with gobs of ridiculous advice, ranging from putting a speaker in your vagina and playing classical music before they're born, to giving them a candy treat for pooping in a toilet. The unfortunate truth is that there are no experts, no authorities, no councils, no government agencies, no churches, no organizations, no non-profits, and no *anybodies* who really know what's best for all children. Just a whole bunch of often bad advice from folks who are guessing, just like you and me. For example, how about this ditty from two 1920s era supposed geniuses, B. G. Jefferis and J. L. Nichols, in their best selling book, <u>Searchlights on Health: The Science of Eugenics</u>:

"Pregnant mothers should avoid thinking of ugly people, or those marked by any deformity or disease; avoid injury, fright and disease of any kind."

And there's a series of other billion-selling parenting guides that are even older, called the Bible, or the Torah, or the Koran, or 50 or more other wonderful fictional variations that may give you some very interesting, yet unproven, child-raising advice. How about this gem, for instance:

Deuteronomy 21:18-21: 'If a man has a stubborn and rebellious son who will not obey the voice of his father or the voice of his mother, and, though they discipline him, will not listen to them, then his father and his mother shall take hold of him and bring him out to the elders of his city at the gate of the place where he lives, and they shall say to the elders of his city, 'This our son is stubborn and

rebellious; he will not obey our voice; he is a glutton and a drunkard.'
Then all the men of the city shall stone him to death with stones. So
you shall purge the evil from your midst, and all Israel shall hear, and
fear."

I'm fairly sure there are better ways to handle discipline, not to mention stoning is still illegal in most countries. Although stoning would be one hell of a deterrent.

Or, you could threaten to send your kids to Sambia, where it is believed that semen is the mojo of manhood. That's a very strange and unsettling story better told by Ogi Ogas in A Billion Wicked Thoughts.

Society has collectively created several rule books that have destroyed several generations of children. We all run around like idiots making sure our children are primed to *succeed.* But what is success?

Success is perhaps the single most subjective word in the English language. To most, success equates to how much money you have, or which school drafted you, or how many songs you've sold on iTunes. Success is identified with one or more people placing you on a pedestal, and treating you as if you are better or more special than everyone else.

And when you've finally realized that you have failed to achieve your unattainable predetermined goals, you become disappointed. It's no wonder why rates of depression are at record levels, albeit we have only recently began to measure it. But what if it's we *parents* who are responsible for cultivating depression? Perhaps it is our fault that we allow our children to engage with mass and social media, creating false norms that are rarely achieved by 99 percent of us. Think about the scenes portrayed in most television comedies and dramas. A large suburban home. Nice clothes. Plenty of food. And a tidy happy ending at the end of every segment. I can personally vouch that's *not* how shit went down in my hood. And let's not even discuss the nightmare of pricey meds and endless therapy.

To clarify, if your child is depressed, it may have been your lack of guidance that caused it. Hey, don't be so tough on yourself, Mom and Dad. No one is perfect. Chemical imbalances are real. But come on – one out of every five Americans has a chemical imbalance that requires therapy or pharmaceutical treatment? That's bordering on ridiculous. Why do Spain, Italy, Israel, Germany, India, Mexico, and South Africa have half the depressed people America has? Japan and China are even better, with a mere 6.6% and 6.5% respectively of their citizens suffering a depressive episode, according to the WHO's World Mental Health Survey Initiative. It's our *culture* that's the difference. And that culture begins with you, Mom and Dad.

Parents should be more realistic about our world, our society, fundamental economic shifts with respect to evolving or receding careers, barriers to entry, the recidivism of the American dream, our hopelessly antiquated American school systems and our lack of investment in them, and time constraints of households with working parents. It's damn near impossible to provide a stable, secure, and enriching home environment that nurtures happiness. Success in life is a harmonious balance between personal happiness and financial stability. That is precisely why I do not advocate free-range parenting, a lack of discipline, trophies for everything, and goals set too low. What I do recommend is a custom tailored plan for personal success. But you can't make that plan until you've projected your future earnings in an unstable economy, and what social impulses in the future will affect your child. Can you see the Catch-22 there?

Back in the olden days, career planning was easy. Throw the kids out on the farm and have them pick some cotton. Or you'd send them to work in the neighborhood mines or factories. For those who had no other viable options, the military would take them and help sort things out in exchange for a few good years of youth. Leaders would sort themselves out, and everyone managed to make a decent living. Obviously, that's not the case today. How can you set the bar when you don't yet know your child's aptitude? You shouldn't push them too hard, but you also should not allow them to fail by leaving them to their own devices.

See what I mean? Parenting is no picnic. No pressure, but remember that the ultimate success or failure of that innocent little life is riding in your hands. There are no second chances. No do-overs. No mulligans. So you'd better get it right, the first time. This here book is the perfect start and assistant. It's time to reboot parenting. Throw away all those fake specialists and their terribly misguided research and advice, and let's rewrite the rules. It all begins with you.

If you're lucky enough to become a parent, one day you will have a startling epiphany. You'll immediately recognize that specific moment, when everything seems to move in slow motion, and then it stops – and you'll suddenly envision illuminated green columns of vertically arranged Asian characters on a computer screen. You may even begin to realize why your über-traditional parents did the things they did. Why they told you the things they told you. Why they disciplined you harshly at times, and why they backed off during others. Why you weren't allowed to go over that certain friend's house while all your other friends were allowed. Why they secretly cut the battery cables in your car the moment they found out you'd met a nice girl named Bambi who offered you a hand-job at that fine "gentleman's bar" down the road. And in the next moment, you will forgive them for their trespasses, as they hopefully have forgiven you yours. You probably had many more. You will develop an entirely new appreciation for the patience and tolerance they displayed, in the face of all the endless bullshit you put them through. You might begin to sift through the remainder of your countless memories for all the other gems that may lay in waiting. And you may just be inspired to pick up the phone or send a card (and not *text*) to deliver a warm and well-deserved "thank you."

My epiphany happened one New Year's Eve as I was becoming painfully aware of my own mortality while watching Dick Clark stumble through one of his last televised celebrations. Like everyone else, I had a list of empty resolutions I was ready to make as the clock struck midnight, knowing damn well I'd break every single one of them by the first of February. Don't lie – you did too.

That night, a very strange man I used to know pondered aloud, unknowingly within earshot of a young pregnant bartender, "She used to be so hot. Why do people have kids?"

You can imagine the rather long, uncomfortable silence that followed. Even the music seemed to quiet for a moment, like in one of those awkward movie moments. You could physically feel heat as the death ray that the very offended bartender cast at this man warmed his beer bottle, before she ever so casually knocked it over, spilling it all over his lap. "Oops," she said. "Must have been that damn *baby* getting in the way. I am so sorry." As he went to the men's room to get some napkins, those of us who knew him laughed heartily. We then simply shook our heads, as usual, and went back to our more normal conversations, with more normal people.

The bartender couldn't have known this man was a textbook psychological disaster. Casting HIPPA to the wind, he openly admitted he had been diagnosed with OCD, ODD, ADD, ADHD, and perhaps every other documented psychological affliction with a "D" in its acronym, as listed in the old-school ICD-9 code range between 290 and 319. This man was proud to admit that he refused meds because they made him "feel funny," as he took another sip of his third vodka and cranberry. Apparently, he was paranoid that the meds he was prescribed might be associated with some of mind-controlling conspiracy. A little too much talk radio in his diet, I surmised.

And yes, his depression was undoubtedly a direct result of his parents. I had the displeasure of meeting his dysfunctional family on a few strange occasions, and I quickly learned they were probably as bad or worse off than he.

I apologized to the pretty pregnant bartender on his behalf. I told her that she was still very hot, and that any other man would gladly date her. I ordered another dirty martini, left a sizable tip, then carefully leaned back on my barstool and pondered the nitwit's naïve question for a long while. The longer I pondered his question, the more I realized his query was not quite as stunted as his mind was.

Obviously, the answer is not an easy one. We're talking about human beings, the single most random species we're currently aware of. Although I consider myself a fairly rational person, I struggled to find an explanation that he, or even a person with average intellect, could easily digest.

The first two answers to his question that came to my mind were *vanity* and *hormones*. But I knew the complete answer had to be much deeper than that. A tangent, several copious bar-related digressions, and a martini or several later, I had my epiphany. I became angry with the entire state of American child rearing. My New Year was ruined. I snuck out of the bar and immediately set off to write this book, for the first of several times.

I learned the hard way that the American dream is bullshit, and hard work has absolutely nothing to do with achieving success. But, work is necessary for survival above public assistance. Unfortunately, it isn't at all uncommon for an average American parent to work two or three shitty jobs simultaneously to avoid the inherent guilt that accompanies complacency, not to mention the fear and discomfort of being homeless. President George W. Bush once publicly lauded a mother for working three jobs. He called it *uniquely American*. I call it ludicrous reality.

As I progressed through public school and adolescence, all I remember are the words *success* and *wealth* repeatedly pounded into my mind, as if my entire generation was entitled to these rare gifts. Of course, in those days, Ronald Reagan was king of the world, Michael Jackson was still black, big hair and leg warmers were in, and everything seemed wonderful. American folks weren't thinking straight in the 80s.

Years later, with radical changes in attitudes and technology, I began to perceive that society was slowing down, becoming lazy, and diverting away from the hard work ethic of prior generations. Ironically, people appeared to be living better than ever. You could own a new home with a wardrobe full of designer clothes, eat gourmet meals, and drive a luxurious car with power windows all without ever breaking a sweat. Some folks I knew lived amazingly well, and they didn't work *at all*. This stark contrast to my norm made me wonder how we could possibly keep training our children to expect the same.

The problem with modern society and its high rates of depression is *normalcy bias* – the phenomenon that occurs when the perceived norm becomes the actual norm. Powerful media conglomerates completely control almost everything we perceive. Since the 1980s, I cannot recall any popular movie, television show, commercial, or rap song that lauds hard work and making ends meet in a ghetto. On television, everyone is rich, wears great clothes, and lives on a one-acre lot in the suburbs. I have to admit, life seemed pretty damn easy. That's what today's children have learned to expect.

Back to the weirdo's question. In this gilded age of birth control, morning-after pills, and over-the-counter pregnancy tests, most Americans don't have children by mistake – they *willingly* reproduce. And there are quite a few reasons why.

One popular reason women have children, although rarely admitted, is for reasons of *vanity*. "Oooh, look at me! Oh, that's my little precious! I'm so special, because I have a *baby*! Yay me!" This pompous narcissistic behavior lasts a couple years, until the brat becomes a mouthy boogie-eating toddler who's really not all that cute anymore. This often prompts the attention-starved mom to immediately pawn child #1 off to daycare and promptly have another baby. She does this to get more attention. This may sound harsh, but it's frequently true. I'm not going to sugar-coat anything in this book, so keep your seat belt on.

I was surprised to learn via a drunken hearsay confession that some women use their ovaries as a weapon of *mass disruption*. From the moment she becomes aware of her reproductive capability, she realizes she can use that weapon to catch a man she feels unworthy of. Or, in an even more deceiving ploy, she can trap a man to extort 18 or more years of unearned and untaxed income in a necessary yet often abused legality known as *child support*. The formula is dreadfully simple. To invoke her deadly weapon, all she has to do is provide some alcoholic beverages, wear a low-cut shirt with a push-up bra, and inconspicuously forget to take her pill for a couple days – and there goes his dream of financial independence.

Insecure women have children because they crave more affection than their lackluster partner is capable of providing. What they fail to realize is that once the child reaches adolescence, he or she transforms into a selfish little bitch, and the affection they once showered upon you painfully transforms into resentment.

Some other women believe their children may provide an insurance policy for old age. It doesn't work that way. There is still no such thing as "parental support." Your children, no matter how much you've done to ensure their lives were entitled and successful, have absolutely zero obligation to care for you – ever. You could be broke and penniless, still paying his or her student loans, living in a box under a dirty and noisy interstate. That biological child you painstakingly raised might become the CEO of the most profitable asteroid mining corporation in the universe someday. It doesn't matter, because he or she will never be legally obligated to give you one single penny – or even acknowledge your existence, for that matter.

On the other hand, most men typically have children for one reason – invariably as a result of *hormonal extortion.* Women are very aware that in the right situation, at the right moment, or at any moment for that matter, most men simply cannot or will not avoid a certain biological temptation.

For either parent, there's always a non-financial "out." If you opt out of the parental situation to pursue your dream of climbing the corporate ladder, that's your choice. There is no law that says you must participate in the raising of your offspring if you choose not to. There are quite a few fathers and mothers I've met who try to skirt all paternal and financial responsibility. There are also parents, usually women, who use their children as a pawn or punishment by not allowing the other parent to participate in parenting.

I am sure you have encountered parents who should have never been allowed to become parents. There is nothing worse than raising an unwanted child in this cruel world. Sure, adoption is always an option. But it's mentally difficult to surrender a child, and the resulting guilt can be psychologically crippling for both the parent and the adopted child. It's ten times easier to buy a gun in most states than it is to get an abortion. The next time you see some childless anti-abortion protestor parading a poster or a license plate, tell them you'll pray that the fruits of their labor will never find them in an ironically adverse situation – like on the wrong side of a gun held by one of those unwanted children raised by a resentful and unprepared parent.

God-forbid your child arrives with a debilitating mental or physical condition. You cannot send her back, and you'll be eternally haunted if you give her up for adoption. I knew a wonderful woman who recently passed in her early 70s. She gave up her career, her marriage, and her life to care for her severely handicapped son. Once her son reached his 40s and had a full-time caretaker, she endeavored to take the first vacation of her life. Even in this scientifically enlightened age of ultrasounds and in-vitro DNA testing, having a healthy child is still a little like Russian roulette.

Ironically, the dimwit who asked "why do people have kids?" might be smarter than all the parents on Earth. Parenting is certainly the most thankless of all jobs. Most first-time parents will not realize this for several years. But now that you're a parent, the *why* no longer matters. You're stuck in the game. Your challenge is to do the right thing – raise your child to become a hard-working and responsible adult, just like your parents raised you.

Remember this one important thing as you ponder slacking as a parent – bad youth become bad adults, and murderous and thieving adult children will make your life miserable, too. Lots of apathetic folks believe the authorities have a handle on bad people, but they're not thinking big picture. It is important to remember that authorities cannot do anything until a crime is actually committed. Every crime requires a victim, and there is always the possibility that *you* could be that first victim. Nip it in the bud, and help avoid this sort of situation. Be like Toya Graham – that mom in Baltimore who was caught smacking her son around when she found him rioting over Freddie Gray in the streets.

You'll need to fight hard in your battle to instill a sense of goodness and responsibility in your child. To me, as to every parent before me since the beginning of American history, it appears American youth is on a downward spiral.

Only this time, it appears to be suspiciously and cleverly engineered.

It is the purpose of this book and my obligation as a parent to make you aware of the potential pitfalls of parenting. Learn from my mistakes and experiences, so that you can raise your own angel.

There is no need to be liked as a parent; if you're looked upon as your child's friend, they'll have zero respect for you. Don't be afraid to be the bad guy – teach them the meaning of the word "no." And when you say it, *mean it.* They'll thank you someday. And more importantly – you'll thank yourself. Don't give your children any more slack than necessary. Human nature persuades us to search for the easy way out in all situations. If we allow this in childhood, it becomes gospel and leads to mediocrity in life. Failure may mean permanently supporting your failed children and their subsequent illegitimate children rather than living a comfortable retirement. Some grandparents voluntarily raise their grandchildren. But that often means those fools are dumb, lonely, or have failed as parents the first time around. From personal experience, I can vouch that Granny and Paps will make those same mistakes a second and even third time.

Thinking back to that night at the bar, although we've touched on many reasons and topics, I still can't find a real answer to that strange man's query. Hormones, lust, vanity, power, insecurity, and loneliness all play a part in the answer, but there's still no catch-all I can possibly phrase in a single sentence to explain why people have kids. Unlike most other mammals, we supposedly have a conscience. I suppose humans are peculiar – or perhaps, just plain clueless.

Regardless of your reasons, be thankful that your parents (or whoever raised you) took the time to teach you to become a responsible adult. I had to figure most of that out on my own. This is the book I wish she would have written for me had she had the opportunity. I hope it fills in any blanks that remain for you. And, most of all, I hope this book begins the process of dismantling years of failed parenting books and advice, because it ain't working. Join me in this reboot of parenting as we all search for truth.

2: it's all up to you

Honestly, being a parent has always scared the devil out of me. It is, without a doubt, the single largest and most important responsibility of your life. The sacrifices you'll need to make in time, energy, and in your finances is tremendous. The most frightening thing is that there are no do-overs. No take-backs. No mulligans. You will only get one chance to mold your helpless little angel into a responsible asset to society. Once he or she is an adult, it's over. Your influence will be done long before that.

How can you guide your child down the right path, to ensure that he or she will eventually become – not necessarily a *success*, whatever that may be – but at least an asset to society? Better put your gloves on, because you've got one hell of a fight on your hands.

There is no unified set of rules or guidelines for becoming a good parent. Humans require training and a license to drive a vehicle. Most states require at least some kind of background check before you can purchase a weapon. You'll need a teaching certificate to become a legitimate teacher in most school systems. Yet no blessing, education, permission, license, or background check is required for the most potentially damaging thing you can do to another person: irresponsibly produce and subsequently raise another human being.

So, what is the *correct* way to raise a child? And who in society gets to make those arbitrary rules? There are thousands of books, YouTube videos, psychologists, psychiatrists, feminists, misandrists, rabbis, priests, clerics, palm readers, consultants, grandparents, aunts, uncles, co-workers, soccer moms, hairdressers and other so-called specialists who all think they know the best way to raise children. The truth is, none of them, myself included, have more than a few hopefully helpful hints.

Each and every child is different, as is each parent, each supporting family, each socioeconomic situation, each environment, and each home setting. There are too many variables to pigeon-hole any one particular method of successful parenting that works for everyone. All those ultra-liberal authors, specialists and psychologists have done a wonderful job of destroying multiple generations of American children since the 1800s. If most of them weren't already dead, perhaps they might take solace in knowing they've successfully made every proven and effective form of verbal and physical discipline illegal, and even the most well-intentioned types of fear unethical. I can imagine the rampant recanting that might be happening today if Benjamin Spock or Lena and William Sadler were still around. We may never know how many millions of children have been damaged or ruined by poor vetted and published parenting advice. Perhaps these *specialists* are beginning to realize their failed efforts constitute a perfected formula for raising limitless numbers of monsters with no goals or aspirations. I suppose those *specialists* have invested their capitalist rewards in gated communities that might temporarily isolate them from the fruit of their errors.

At best, all we've got are parenting generalizations, passed down from folks who have made mistakes, and theories from those who have yet to make them. As a parent, you have to do the best you can with a little common sense and any knowledge you can wrap your hands around.

Think about it, Murica. When was the last time a good-ol' blonde-haired blue-eyed all-American bubba named *Bob*,

Mike, or *Jimmy* won a national spelling bee? Or a science fair? Or a math contest? Or a chess contest? Or any non-sports contest which has anything to do with being smart, clever, or innovative? I'll tell you. It was 2007, when Evan O'Dorney, from Danville, California, won the Scripps National Spelling Bee. Ubiquitous among the winners since then are names like Sriram, Ansun, Mishra, Shivashankar, Veeramani, Sukanya, Snigdha, and Mahankali. Kids from immigrant families who a generation or two ago never dreamed they would call America home are beating the pants off your ten-plus generation all-American bubbas. And they're beating them badly.

Before you run off and scream *racist*, I should mention that my own parents were Iron Curtain immigrants. And, as a matter of fact, this here first-gen 'Murican came in as a runner-up in the Philadelphia Spelling Bee preliminaries in 1978. So shut your pie-hole, you Prius driving bitch.

Have American kids lost their edge? It sure looks that way. But why? And what can you do about it? You can begin by putting those hunting rifles, tennis rackets, fishing poles, golf clubs, fantasy football picks, tabloids, reality shows, and spa VIP cards away – and beginning to take your parental responsibility dead seriously. It's all about culture, and apparently, we've fucked ours up royally. And that's what this reboot is all about. We can learn much about being successful parents from other cultures.

Immigrant parents seem to hold on to more traditional child-rearing customs and practices, some of which would be considered harsh by current standards. Shame, guilt, and fear were three very effective elements of my first-generation immigrant upbringing. High on discipline and low on tolerance, these immigrant parents provide a wonderful model for raising future doctors, scientists, and other worthy professionals. Make fun of them all you want, but they'll be eating your pie until Juan, DeShawn, and Bobby – our former Hispanic, African-American, and Caucasian all-Americans – graduate into the new lower-class *minority*. If America continues on her current course, by the year 2030, seventy to eighty percent of all Caucasian, Hispanic, and African-American children will be performing low-wage labor, if they're employed at all, for the foreign accent-bearing masters they once taunted in school.

How well you do as a parent will be critically important to *your* future, as well as your child's. There is only so much you can do as a parent, but the repercussions of failure are frightening. For example, if your child eventually succumbs to criminal desires, your good name will be tarnished, along with theirs. After all, it was your job to teach that child morals and common sense. If your daughter has poor judgment, leading to illegitimate children, you may find it necessary to raise your grandchildren as your own, incurring an additional 18 or more years of time and financial responsibility that you likely didn't plan for. Of course, you could deny your child's children, But could you live with the fact that if something adverse happened to those innocent grandkids, you had foregone the opportunity to save them? Not to mention the heartbreak of seeing your own children fail in life, something you could have prevented with a little more time, attention, or guidance. You will only get one chance per child, and I remind you, there are no do-overs. So make it count.

You will get tired, angry and frustrated, so make sure you've always got a backup plan. Keep a stable of responsible babysitters, or have a friend or parent step in when you feel you're about to lose your cool. When you start to feel overwhelmed, take a nap or see a movie. Take some time to readjust. Frustration happens quite frequently, especially as your children get older.

There are a few consistent rules that seem to apply, no matter your race, color, creed, education, political persuasion, income level, music preference, religion, Mac or PC preference, or favorite perfume. I've peppered this book with these simple rules. Using this information as your foundation, eventually, you too will come up with your own missing parenting reboot manual.

Remember, even from the earliest age, they're carefully watching and cataloging everything you do. If you smoke, drink, steal, cuss, pierce your own nipples, sleep around recklessly, or beat your mate, you've just molded your child's mind with the fact such behavior is normal and acceptable. Chances are mini-me will become a chip off the old block. In twenty years, when that child becomes a certifiable screw-up, you'll have no one to blame but yourself.

Up until this point, this book has been the epitome of doom and gloom. But there are good times along with the bad. People ask me if being a parent is fun. Sometimes it really is fun. To me, there's nothing like realizing the firsts and recognizing that you were the catalyst for that first. And kids do say the darndest things. You never know what's going to come out of their mouth. For others, things may be different. It depends who you are, and what your situation entails. Some folks simply aren't cut out for this type of responsibility.

But is parenting *rewarding?* There is a certain element of pride you'll feel at times that comes from watching your child's successes. But this depends on how critical you are, and what you consider to be successes.

Parenting is also challenging, tiring, frustrating, and depressing. If I had the opportunity to measure the overall positive versus negative parental experiences on a mathematical scale, I can honestly attest that a normal ratio would probably be a 3:1 ratio, with the former being positive. And I work damn hard at parenting, spending a disproportionate amount of my spare time, and invoking a tremendous volume of filtering and reverse psychology to achieve that level of happiness. Anyone who tells you it takes anything less is a sociopathic liar, spends a little too much time on medication, is still waiting for Jesus to fill in the blanks. For me, it's that positive experience that makes life worthwhile.

3: ppd: pre-partum delight

Summer just got pregnant. That's not her real name, but it might as well be, according to the website personalnameology.com. Visit it yourself, and you'll get the gist. It's surprisingly accurate. Summer is twenty-ish, and this is her first pregnancy. Like millions of other young women in Summer's shoes, she climbed to the top of the highest digital hill she could find (Instagram?) and yelled at the top of her lungs, "HEY WORLD! I'M PREGNANT! PAY ATTENTION TO MEEEEE!" Summer then set her social networking security settings to nil and opened her entire life to anyone who would listen.

Summer is completely stereotypical: acting and reacting exactly like every other young pregnant girl I've ever come across. I correctly predicted she'd announce her pregnancy before the end of her first trimester. Most medical practitioners will agree this is a big no-no, simply because the viability of the fetus is not quite established at this early stage. Lots of unfortunate things happen during the first trimester, including dreadful miscarriages. But this did not deter Summer. She bought her unborn child several children's' books. She set up her own gift registry. Summer even scheduled an ultrasound, in the back of a van, in a shopping mall parking lot, for the sole purpose of choosing the color of her baby's room.

During her cinematic adventure, Summer's mood swings made her as unpredictable as Lindsey Lohan during her darkest days. I felt pain for her poor, poor husband of only a few months. A law enforcement officer's life is stressful enough without the constant nagging of a young, insanely clingy pregnant wife. Tony is on Facebook too, and he did everything he could to bite his digital tongue.

No matter how many times Summer hacked Tony's account, publicly displaying her displeasure with his typically male decisions to do things like dare play a round of golf or have a beer with the boys while she was carrying his then alien-looking embryo, Tony seemed to remain a perfect gentleman. If you've ever heard the old tales about cravings for pizza, pickles and ice cream at three in the morning, I can personally attest that those are absolutely true. Tony did exactly what he was expected to do as a doting father-to-be – he massaged her, soothed her spirits, and satisfied her insane cravings (probably at higher than normal speeds with police lights blaring) no matter the hour. Tony deserves no less than a Nobel Prize for dealing with nine full months of Summer's hormonal torture.

A few months down the road from Summer's announcement came the traditional baby shower. A woman usually gets one really good baby shower, and only for her first child. Most of us old pros realize that interest and turnout begins to wane with subsequent children. By the time a woman has her third kid, her baby shower is normally nothing more than heading to Target alone for a Starbucks and a quick shopping trip. But the first baby shower is a huge rite of passage for a new mother. And her friends had better arrive in a minivan filled with presents. The shower is kind of like a young mother's coming-out party. After all, this is proof-positive to her mother, family, friends, neighbors, parishioners, co-workers, strangers, enemies, and the rest of the world that she is good enough to produce something that'll shit its pants for at least two full years.

Future dads used to be excluded from these dreadful events. However, today's *more sensitive* fathers are expected to participate and sometimes even be involved in the planning stages of a baby shower. According to one husband, in his own words, that completely validated his decision to have a vasectomy after his first planned child.

In a nutshell, Summer had her baby. And a few short months later, her husband had enough. Summer has now joined the single mom army. Tony had a vasectomy and is now dating childless blondes.

Scientists are on the threshold of proving that there is some sort of chemical switch that fundamentally changes a woman's personality the moment she becomes pregnant for the first time. More often than not, men believe it's a *crazy switch*.

A Connecticut woman, 34-year-old Miriam Carey, was shot to death by police after a car chase that began when she tried to breach a barrier at the White House. Her mother said she suffered from post-partum depression. She was traveling with her 1-year-old baby girl when she rammed the barrier. Fortunately, the baby avoided serious injury.

Michael and Maria seemed to have the perfect marriage. The high school sweethearts and best friends did everything together. Maria completely supported everything Michael wanted to do, and Michael worked hard to make all her dreams come true. They were so affectionate that it was, at times, sickening. Both Michael and Maria were working, combining their incomes to buy a home and pay off some student debt and wedding loans. About a year after they had their "perfect" $30,000 wedding (incredibly foolish in my opinion, yet quite typical in most northeastern states), Maria decided it was time to have children. Just as if they were characters in a tidy chick lit novel, exactly nine months later, they had a perfect little girl. And that's where their fairytale ended.

Three months after the birth of their daughter, Maria was pregnant again. She announced that she had decided to become a stay-at-home mom. Michael was caught by surprise, but he agreed to get a second and third job to grant Maria's wish. Maria had a few friends who lived in the suburbs with large houses and new cars. Suddenly, Maria decided Michael should provide these things for her, too. Being a man of meager means, these new demands began to put undue stress on their relationship. But Michael worked as hard as he could, with the goal in mind of satisfying Maria's every whim. A year later, they had a second child, adding an additional financial burden to Michael's already troubled situation.

Maria became impatient. Michael became stressed. Maria, at the behest of her mother, took their two children and moved back in with her well-to-do parents, in their suburban home, until Michael could "get his act together." Michael was shell-shocked and heartbroken. He moved back in with his parents and saved every dollar he could, until he was able to afford a humble home in a better part of the city. It wasn't the suburbs, but it wasn't all that bad. But that wasn't good enough, and Maria asked for a divorce.

Maria had fundamentally changed. But how, and why? To this day, Maria blames it on her parents who pressured her to leave what they determined was an underperforming husband. Michael believes it was more of a chemical change that happened suddenly after the birth of her first child. Maria did not realize any change, but I and other outsiders saw it too. She had a completely different post-partum personality. Was it really a chemical imbalance, or was it another parental failure? It's hard to tell, but it sure smells like the latter.

Darrell retired from the armed services after 20 years and married a sweetheart he'd met in the Philippines. They had a beautiful little girl when they returned to the states. Everything was wonderful, Darrell was happy, and life was great. Darrell told me they'd have sex so much it hurt, even after their first child was born. Two years later, Sandy had a second child. Soon after the birth, Sandy too seemed to go batty. She went from being a sexual dynamo to an arctic freeze. She was mean, depressed, and often downright evil. About a year later, Darrell could no longer take the physical and mental abuse. Darrell found greener pastures and split. In Sandy's case, she was unaffected by the birth of her first child. Her hormonal change happened only after child number two.

Josh's son's mother flipped dramatically after his child's birth. I wouldn't consider Josh a "needy" person, but he does enjoy his space. But before Kristin had her baby, she used to drive three hours to spend the night at home with Josh, rather than staying in a hotel, and then drive three hours back to work the next morning. Just weeks after Kristin's maternity leave was over, she started spending the night in a hotel 45 minutes away, because it was "too inconvenient" to drive home.

Josh was completely confused. They just had this beautiful child that Kristin begged to have, and now she didn't want to be with him? It didn't really bother Josh that Kristin spent her nights in a hotel, although Josh later learned Kristin was having an affair. What Josh said really sucked about his situation was that their son wouldn't sleep through the night for two full years, and Josh had to deal with that alone.

A few years later, after Josh's son finally decided it was better to sleep through the night, Kristin decided she no longer wanted to be married. She asked if Josh wanted to go to counseling. He declined, and she admitted to him that that she didn't want to either. The woman Josh married nine years prior seemed to have been abducted by aliens during childbirth and replaced by this complete stranger who looked just like her. As Josh packed up what was left of his life and scoured local apartments for a place to live, he asked Kristin, "What happened to us?" She replied, "I guess I changed."

Tony, Michael, Darrell, and Josh – it's not you, fellas. I will gladly vouch for all of you. This kind of drastic hormonal change thing is very real, and it happens more often than you'd think. Some doctors blame it on post-partum depression, with about 1 in 8 women developing this debilitating mental condition in days to months after the birth of a child. Hormone levels suddenly drop to pre-pregnancy levels, and apparently that's a huge bummer.

Perhaps, depending on the woman and her mindset – and this will undoubtedly anger every misandrist in the solar system – the biggest single contributing factor to her depression might be that she's no longer a *princess* once she has given birth. Now, instead of being cherished and lauded by friends and family, she's just another plain old girl with a screaming poop machine. Think of it like a celebrity who has just fallen out of favor after having her ass kissed for decades. It must suck, right? She sits around at home, staring at the mirror, wondering why no one's calling or making a fuss over her. Eventually, she ends up drinking and finds herself in an embarrassing situation, which results in a tabloid cover. After she's gone completely batshit crazy, people become interested in her again, and the cycle repeats.

My advice? If you like your life the way it is, don't change anything. If you're a man, have a vasectomy and adopt an orphan. You'll be saving your own sanity, your partner's sanity, and perhaps your relationship too. And you may even save a needy child from an uncertain future.

Ladies, reboot your child making decision tree. Make sure you're doing things for the right reasons, and ensure your relationship is strong enough to handle the sudden changes that may occur.

4: vagina barf

"Oooh, it's so amazing! It's the most beautiful thing I have ever seen!" Said no one, ever.

But, according to Miss Manners, that's what you're supposed to say when someone asks you what it was like to see that blood and mucous covered child slide out of your hyperextended vagina. Frankly, it's more like extreme period chunks mixed with vagina barf. Seriously, think cheap dog food. It's plain nastiness. The birth process is not for the faint of heart.

You have to feel for Mom. Thirty-six weeks or so have passed since you accepted his seed. Your skin has been stretched to its limits, your hormones are going ballistic, and you're scrambling to shave hair or squeeze pimples that have never appeared *there* before. You'll literally feel like you're about to pop. It's probably been at least three months since you and your partner were intimate. A few token hand jobs are probably not enough to disguise the fact that the woman he found hot enough to sleep with and take the chance of impregnating nine months ago is now much heavier, sweatier, more miserable, quite moody, and probably puking in the brand new Subaru station wagon that you forced him to purchase because, after all, the commercials say that Subaru is supposedly *love*.

Don't worry, dad. Paternal regret is completely normal at this stage. And it will also be common at several stages in the future of your parental adventure.

You, as the mom-to-be, are past most of the excitement generated by all the fuss. Now, you just want that giant seven pound alien being out of your gut. You have taken over Daddy's favorite chair, because it's the only place you won't bitch about being uncomfortable. The rule is – if she has to suffer, so does he.

In the movies, it goes like this. All of the sudden, usually at the most inconvenient time possible, and always in public, you may feel unusually wet down there. What a mess. Hold the press! Stop everything! Call the address book! Your water just broke! Never you mind the disgusting mess of DNA and bodily fluid, including mucus, urine, bacteria, sometimes poop, and even more fun stuff that just destroyed his favorite chair – he'll tend to that later. It's always better to give it a day or two to fester. For now, you'd better drop everything, because it's time for your spotlight moment; the normal person's equivalent to winning an Academy Award. Roll your fat ass into that new Subaru, and drive like hell to the hospital. This might be the only time you could potentially get a pass for blowing that senseless stop sign at the end of your street with a *California Roll*, so use caution, but have at it.

Honestly, it's rare that your water will break before actual labor. And if your amniotic sac does rupture before you get to the hospital, it's usually not a gush, but more like a trickle. What you'll typically feel are unbearable cramps caused by contractions less than a minute apart. That's what sends most moms to the delivery ward.

These days, the father is expected to be present during the birthing process. That means Daddy has to prepare for the birth too in a very unnatural establishment known as Lamaze class. Supposedly, these classes help pregnant women understand how to cope with pain, in ways that both facilitate labor and promote comfort, including the initiation of strange breathing motions that were probably engineered for no other reason than to take your mind off that pain. He'll have to suck it up, bring his pillow, and check his attitude at the door. At 6 PM every Wednesday night, for six painful weeks, he will be forced to sit in a

Yoga room, holding his woman's hand and emulating her breathing, along with eight other very pussy-whipped men.

Jon was present during the birth of his daughter over 20 years ago. Sure, he was snookered into the Lamaze thing the first time around too. But during his daughter's birth, something went wrong. The monitoring hardware indicated that they had lost the fetal heartbeat at some point during the early stages of labor. "Sir, you'll have to wait out here," said the masculine looking, morbidly obese medical practitioner as she grabbed Jon's shoulder and pushed him out of the room with protruding beer belly, closing the door in his face. Jon very loudly and repeatedly asked what the deal was, but was shooed away. Jon yelled loudly as hospital security quickly approached to investigate the situation. They were no help.

Jon's daughter's biological life-giving vessel (if you knew her, you wouldn't give her the courtesy of the title mother) endured an emergency Caesarian section. For those of you who are unfamiliar with this procedure, it's essentially major surgery that involves cutting mom's abdomen open, slicing open her uterus, manually plucking out the child, then stitching it all back together – sometimes resulting in an unforgiving vertical rather than horizontal scar that will forever ruin any hope of a six-pack. One fitness-psycho mother I spoke with actually expressed verbal anger towards her eight-year-old daughter for causing this permanent affliction.

In normal "natural" childbirth, the seven or eight-pound baby stretches and tears the dickens out of Mom's vagina in a nasty sometimes hours-long process. In the event that the baby is positioned incorrectly, or if the umbilical cord wraps around the baby's neck, or any other strange life-threatening malady occurs, your doctors will quickly convert from natural to unnatural as they Caesarian your baby out to protect both baby and mom.

There's a new scary trend starting to pop up in upper socioeconomic areas. Many folks are now opting to have the birthing process *at home*. It's a nouveaux way for moms to attract even more attention as they sail back into the fond traditions of generations past. I'm all about natural remedies, especially better nutrition and exercise and less prescription drugs. But, in this situation, I hope these idiots are within five minutes of a hospital, because both of my children might have died if he were that selfish. My son spent some time in the neonatal intensive care unit. I remember wondering why my son was gasping for air and turning blue soon after he was born. Apparently, he was choking on his own poo. Fortunately, they were able to clear his airway and pickle him with antibiotics to avoid his catching pneumonia. He spent several days in the ICU. He's a strapping young man today, but he may not have had that opportunity had he been born at home. Think about all that could go wrong before you let your hipster-self make that potentially fatal decision.

If you truly love your newborn son, don't overlook the problem of legal torture. Apparently, male infants are not protected against cruel and unusual punishment by the Eighth Amendment to the United States Constitution. So the decision is left up to you – to circumcise, or not to circumcise? Why? Why not? What's the point? The real question is, would you let some heartless doctor cut skin off *your* most private parts? Of course not. That's got to be incredibly painful. So why would you *pay* someone to do that to your innocent little boy? Doctors will systematically recommend this minor surgery to fleece insurance companies for as much as they can. Many doctors don't give an anesthetic before performing a circumcision. And since it technically is a surgery, there are associated risks including blood loss and infection. Why not engage in female genital mutilation and slice the vulva off girls while you're at it? Circumcision removes the natural foreskin on the shaft of the penis, leaving that little "head" part that looks like a mushroom exposed. When a male achieves an adult erection, you can still see the scars on the shaft. Circumcision is an irreversible procedure. You can't easily duct tape that foreskin back on when he's 24. You never know – foreskins might become as cool as iPhones once were. Personally, if I were a man, I would have preferred a choice.

While circumcising two-week-old David Reimer with an electro-cautery needle in Manitoba in 1965, the attending urologist accidentally burned off David's entire penis. This isn't as difficult as you'd think – infant parts are all very tiny, and there's not much room for error. No worries, said the urologist – we'll just give him estrogen shots and tell him he's a girl. So the kid grows up wondering why she's mentally and physically different than her fellow Brownies until her parents told her the truth. She decided to become a boy again. Long story short, he killed himself before his 40th birthday.

Some religious proponents believe a clean penis is holier. But if your god or their god didn't want men to have a foreskin, why did he or she or it put it there? Was that some kind of cruel joke played by a god who hates infants? Some misinformed old-wives in the medical community justify circumcision as helpful from a sanitary perspective, potentially avoiding infection from bacteria that can hide beneath the foreskin. But you can have bacterial cheese under your arms or under your boobs too, and we don't routinely cut those off. More learned opponents propose that circumcision is a silly, painful, cruel, and dated ritual with unfounded roots in religion that can adversely affect the sensitivity of the penis during sexual intercourse. The bottom line? If you don't circumcise him, and teach your son to wash his penis thoroughly, he shouldn't have an issue. Think about it, discuss it with your partner, and choose for your newborn son conscientiously.

You'll tend to overdress your baby in a silly blue or pink outfit and proudly parade her out of the hospital for everyone to see. As you secure the countless straps on your shiny new baby seat to the back seat of your shiny new Subaru, you'll be mentally preparing yourself for the endless stream of paparazzi that will inundate your life for the next few weeks. Daddy or partner may begin scheming as to how he/she can use this time to golf, hunt, or play cards with the fellas, but his bubble will quickly burst as you formally notify him that he will be expected to be immediately available at your every beck and call. And no, he still can't have his La-Z-Boy back just yet.

Since everything in America is now grown with strange hormones or with genetically altered substances, it's no longer allowable to use, *gasp, cow's milk,* to nurture your pristine infant. Even the baby formula you grew up with is being replaced by a nasty, odorless, nearly colorless liquid streaming out of Momma's own udders. Ladies, remember all the times your various sexual partners nibbled on your nipples and nothing came out? From this point forward, they'll never seem quite the same and may be permanently off-limits for non-munchkins. Your cute, adorable, helpless little angel will be suckling on your nips for sustenance, day and night, for the next several months. Prepare for crusty and painful nipples.

Oh, and sex? Fuhget about it. Daddy better find a quiet place with some dirty magazines and a box of tissues, because the pleasure palace shall be closed indefinitely. Mom will casually remind Dad that something the size of a small turkey just came out of her formerly tiny vagina, and that her love hole was stretched and ripped to about twenty times its normal size. She may have had to have it snipped open a bit more to fully allow that 8 pounder to squeeze out, and the resulting stitches will take some time to heal. That's called an *episiotomy*, in case you happen to overhear that term at a Mary Kay party, gentlemen. Google it.

There is the possibility that tiny love canal he fondly remembers may now seem as wide as the Holland Tunnel. Trust me, if he's not hung like a horse, he will feel inadequate banging around in a canyon when he is used to being hugged firmly in a tiny crevice. Men feel inadequate if they feel small, ladies, and that leads to all kinds of mental issues later down the line. If stitches are an option, you might want to elect that.

Remember the man cave? You know, the "office" where he pretended to work while he was really fucking off on FanDuel or shooting video game zombies? It's quite likely that former cave has been repossessed via an undocumented and more domestic form of eminent domain, painted (reluctantly, and probably by him) in some awful pastel color Mom chose specifically so he would never want to move back in. There might even be birds, balloons, flowers and all kinds of other frilly things adorning the walls, where his college degree and baseball trophies used to live. Here's hoping your garage is air conditioned.

You'd both better get used to terms like *Onesies, Diaper Genie, Huggies, and Wipies*. If your poor son has been circumcised, you'll need to apply some kind of antibiotic cream to his poor little wee-wee, so that it won't become infected or result in his scabbing sticking to his diaper. The bottom line is, for at least the next two years, you'll be exposed to blood, pus, snot, poop, piss, puke, and all kinds of other nastiness no one ever talks about or warned you about. If you're the squeamish type, it certainly won't be a picnic.

Enjoy.

5: jesus mary and joseph

Apparently, an old neighbor of mine was very into some guy named *Jesus*. That name isn't too typical in English-speaking American circles, so I assumed her *Jesus* guy might have been Mexican, or perhaps Puerto Rican, where the name *Jesus* is somewhat common. Wait – it couldn't be a Christian thing, could it? Nah. Her bumper stickers and Facebook posts were always neatly coordinated and quite often mentioned things like *Jesus saves. Jesus forgives. Jesus provides.* Jesus this, Jesus that, Jesus everything. At one point I thought, *Wow, that Mexican kid Jesus must be one hell of a handyman.* Apparently, the one thing Super Jesus couldn't do was reach out and smack this silly woman on her forehead for deciding to curse her son for life with a ridiculously obscure biblical name. We're talking Old Testament here – filled with the truly peculiar names that nearly no one has used in millennia. Granted, there are some pretty hipster Old Testament names including Moses, Noah, and Adam. But these fools today are using the more crazy non-trending ones like Solomon, Silas, Titus, Abel, Caleb, and *Balthazar*. Yeah, she went there. She actually named her kid *Balthazar*. Don't be surprised if there's a *Lucifer* in your kid's daycare.

Your parents chose your first name for a reason. In their infinite wisdom, they probably picked a standard name, like Bob, Ted, John, Mary, or Jenny. The year of your birth and your parents' religious background are the average parents' two most influential decision criteria. The year factor pertains to the movie stars or television show characters, musicians, politicians, or fictional characters whose names were popular the year of your birth. This explains the current onslaught of Beyonces, Baracks, and

Britneys that have been born in the past decade. Overwhelming evidence of a complete lack of originality will be revealed, which will more often than not pass on to you environmentally and/or genetically.

Naming a child with a biblical or religious moniker helps those poor creationist parents feel at least some of their worldly sins will be forgiven and bring them a step closer to those pearly gates when their eagerly anticipated demise arrives. Think of it like a favor to God. In both cases, the overwhelming evidence of your complete lack of originality will be revealed, which will more often than not pass on to your children both environmentally and genetically. I must admit that at times I do envy religious naiveté. It must be wonderful to be carefree and apathetic, thinking you don't ever have to do anything meaningful, because you know in your heart with absolutely no doubt that some bearded white man in the sky is taking care of everything with a master plan we simply cannot comprehend. All we have to do is say thanks once a week, eat a terrible tasting wafer that represents human flesh, and ask for forgiveness whenever we make a mistake. I'll be in confession for at least six weeks apologizing for the former paragraph, but it's all good. The handyman will forgive me.

The problem with these obscure names is that most children outside of your tidy little circle won't necessarily share your joy and creativity. Many children (not yours, of course) are cruel and insecure. The first thing an insecure person will do is deflect attention away from him or herself, by any means possible, and then laugh hysterically to engage other weak-minded people to validate and cement that deflected attention. The bully's joke just became a permanent label for your poorly named *Balthazar*, who will forever henceforth be known as *Ball Sucker*.

Considering your child may be stuck in the same school with that insecure idiot and his or her posse for up to twelve years, I'm sure you can deduce that your child will take one hell of a mental beating, quite possibly leading to a deep resentment from which he or she won't easily be able to recover without substantial therapy. That's right – he'll be *depressed*. And his resentment towards your choice will forever affect his relationships, his education, his career, and ultimately his entire outlook on life. Guess whose fault that was? Other than a circumcision, the first name you choose for your child is the only curse you can bestow upon him or her forever. It's critical that you choose that name as wisely as you can.

When choosing a first name, do the "rhyme test" and the "acronym test." For example, *Bob the Slob, Smella Bella,* and *Fatty Patty* are a few of the more juvenile examples of potentially embarrassing or often inappropriate rhymes which your child may be subjected to for several painful years. Please consult a rhyming dictionary or website with your potential first names before committing to them. Rhymezone.com is a good place to start.

Before Miso knew his son was going to be a son, he was fooling around with different female names. He had always liked the name *Paige,* and his mother liked the name *Isabella* for her middle name. They did the rhyme test and decided there wasn't anything serious the kid couldn't overcome. Page, pager, rage, cage; whatever. The name passed the rhyme test easily. *Isabella* might be a bit more challenging with words like *smella* or *fella.* Still, no big deal, because it's a middle name. But after combining the three initials, using Miso's last name, they realized that would have created a disastrous monogramming situation. The initials, Paige Isabella Grey, would have spelled the word

PIG. Imagine the shame and embarrassment having those initials embroidered on her little pee-wee soccer bag. Had Miso not done the *acronym* test, his poor little piglet might have been on Prozac by the age of six.

There are several other obviously negative three-letter words and acronyms you can form using people's initials that you might want to avoid, like:

- *Corey Underwood Mitchell*
- *David Isaac Christiansen*
- *Kalani Karl Kokopeli*
- *Darnell Ignatio Estevez*
- *Zachary Ian Tate*
- *Daniel Ulleses Melfi*
- *Robert Anthony Terrel*
- *Steven Olaf Bennett*
- *George Allen Shaw*
- *Brian Adam Denado*
- *Hannah Olivia Raymond*
- *Bella Uma Madriss*
- *Sadie Isabella Neri*

Always check the combined initials of your child's first, middle, and last names before committing that name to that birth certificate.

Proper coaching before your child gets to school can alleviate or desensitize much of the embarrassment and stress that may accompany an already issued unfortunate name. Bullies look for weakness and tend to avoid strong personalities. A great comeback can shut a bully down permanently. It also doesn't hurt if your kid is a mean looking 6'2" by the time he's 14. Properly prescribed doses of HGH work surprisingly well. I'll discuss that and other secrets in my next book, *Parental Cheats*.

There's also the legal option, which is often less costly and troublesome than a psychiatrist. Unfortunately, you have to be considered an adult by a court to legally change your own name, but a cool parent can help a suffering child.

Many people don't realize that when you name your child, you are providing clues into your personality as a parent, and subsequently providing clues into the make-up of your child's personality. Law enforcement, marketing companies, potential employers, co-workers, bullies, priests, and even possible mates are judging you and sizing you up using all the information at their disposal. And the easiest piece of data that's readily available is your first name. It's on your uniforms, phones, shirts, stickers, bags, license plates, ID badges, books, forms, tattoos, and a hundred other obvious places. And if it isn't readily available, you'll be considered rude if you don't give it up when any stranger asks you for it.

It was supposed to be a book, but Miso Grey never finished it. So rather than waste away on his hard drive, Miso posted his first name analysis for free at personalnameology.com. With nothing more than your first name, Miso posits he can at least guess your strengths and weaknesses – if not uncover your hidden wants and innermost desires. With this information as a basis, marketers believe they are well aware that they may be able to compel you to buy something. Or, although it seems like quite a stretch, Miso believes the clues your first name holds could give someone enough information to find the right words and cause you to fall in love. Think about it, for a moment. If a grown woman's name is along the lines of *Julie*, *Helen*, or *Susan*, she's probably an uptight woman who most likely works as an accountant or an office manager. However, if that woman's name happens to be something like *Britney*, *Ashley*, or *Summer*, she undoubtedly wears a thong and will eventually be found pole dancing on a stage somewhere. It's not pure science at all, and his descriptions are often vague wide of the mark, but you have to agree that a first name is a very good basis to begin an informal subjective psychological evaluation.

If a mother chooses a religious name like "Grace", "Faith", or "Mary" for her child, chances are that child had a strong religious upbringing. If her mom chose a more conservative name like "Helen" or "Nancy," chances are her parents were conservative, and naturally that trait will both genetically and artificially be passed on. Grey states that Helen is the most frigid name in his book. And if you're a man thinking of dating a Kim, Heather, Melissa, or Hannah, you'd better bring a condom.

Nate Silver and Allison McCann created a wonderful chart titled How to Tell Someone's Age When All You Know Is Her Name based off the Social Security Administration index files. At the time of their article, they accurately extrapolated that the average Joshua is about 22, while the average Donald is pushing 60. Emily is most likely in her late teens now, while her great-grandmother Dorothy is breaking Social Security's reserves by living more than 75 years. Silver and McCann have validated that American names are trendy.

Another naming convention that's a hint into someone's mental capacity is the spelling of your given name. For example, some parents think they're being avant-garde by alternating the spelling of a name, which, in some cases, could potentially display originality and forward thinking. Unfortunately, ignorance abounds. Although probably warned by a more sharp hospital employee, they still proceeded to misspell the kid's name (think "Temptress" rather than "Tempest") and force her to deal with the lifetime of bullshit that will accompany that easily correctable mistake. In some cases, depending on her environment, she'll be proud and confident. In most cases, however, the misspellers aren't on the advantageous end of the socioeconomic ladder, which will most likely produce a child who is angry, resentful; or, in the best case for all of us, equally as aloof as her parents.

Today, people blindly make up names. They unknowingly screw up the lives of their helpless children. Miso Grey imagines people Scrabble letters on a table, seeing where they land, and coming up with wackadoo combinations of letters and/or characters, including backslashes and hashtags, ultimately creating some crazy name, in a poor effort to be cute. There is no other way one could explain such silly names like *ShaMichael, JaMiracle, KeyShawn, Bobmarleymon, Younique,* or *V8.* Some of the effects of such poor decisions are categorized and measured in *The Causes and Consequences of Distinctively Black Names,* a research paper written by author and economist Steven Levitt and Roland G. Fryer Jr., an economist and professor from Harvard University. Naming a kid with an uncommon or blatantly ethnic name is brutally selfish on the parents' part, and there's nothing the child can do about it until long after the damage has been done.

Of course, there is a one in a billion chance that he or she becomes a celebrity or a professional athlete, somehow adding a misguided temporary legitimacy to his or her unusual name. That name will propagate for a generation or two before people wonder where the soon to be irrelevant name *D'Brickashaw* originated.

If you are absolutely hell-bent on choosing a creative name, do your child a big favor and save that silly, edgy, misspelled, or biblical moniker for his *middle* name. This way, he can at least abbreviate it when he becomes an atheist and realizes how selfish his parents were. Then, he can lie and say "Solomon" is really "Sal." Sorry, buddy, but there's not much anyone can do for *Balthazar.* Perhaps, like *Barack*, he could go with *Barry* and hope he doesn't become president.

6: what does she do all day?

For thousands of years, Mom's job was to stay in the cave to raise her hairy Neanderthal imps while Fred and Barney went out to slay wooly mammoths to put food on the table. More recently, there began a movement in which some mothers are trying to re-justify this behavior, trying to get back to the "good old days" in their make-believe effort to save the world. They've even come up with a catchy acronym for their stay-at-home movement: *SAH*.

There is a fundamental problem with the current SAH theology. Yesterday's SAH moms didn't have dishwashers, washing machines, vacuum cleaners, disposable diapers, walk-in clinics, Walgreens, Target, Amazon Prime, Molly Maids, daycare, playdates, tennis, golf carts, bocce, Facebook, Twitter, Netflix, Chinese nail salons, or whatever other distractions I can't practically imagine that keep SAHs occupied eight to ten hours a day. Back in the day, before all the modern conveniences, women had to work hard as "housekeepers." God forbid you call a stay-at-home mom a "housekeeper" today – you might get slapped, because that's now an insult. Think *stewardess* versus *flight attendant*. Yeah, it's that insulting.

Most of today's stay-at-home moms fall into one or more of the following categories:

- *Lazy*
- *Unemployable*
- *Spoiled and showing off*
- *A victim of a controlling husband*

We'll take an in-depth look at all four situations. But first, in Mom's defense, were you aware the United States of America is the only industrialized nation that does not legally mandate paid maternity leave? Even *China* gives you 90 days. I can attest that those the first few months are immensely difficult. The countless diaper changes, middle of the night feedings, sleep issues, and everything else that little brat needs all require constant care, which is exhausting. I met a new mother at a cocktail party who asked me to hold her three-month old baby for a moment, had a few drinks, and left her child with me for at least an hour before she returned to the party realizing she forgot something.

I have to admit, after six to nine months, it's more than likely that the average stay-at-home mom will be home chillaxin' while her new baby is napping for hours on end. Or, she'll pawn her child off for several hours to *develop social skills* at some boutique daycare. The stay-at-homes in my community even have a tidy little group on Facebook. I joined it under a pseudonym to see what was going on. The most important posts in their group appear to be when the next Thirty-One Gifts party is, or who can recommend a good cleaning lady.

Socioeconomically disadvantaged mothers have usually thrown in the towel regarding work and career. These moms have little to no access to anything or anyone who can help them, and no opportunity to advance in their careers. With child care costs eclipsing many lower wage positions, it's often economically wiser for mothers not to work. Break-even situations can be advantageous in terms of work experience, medical benefits, networking, and social development. But if working is a financially unfavorable proposition, which is occurring more frequently today due to our economic environment with outsourcing and automation, hopefully this type of SAH mother will take full advantage of this opportunity to help her child advance. No, that does not mean not letting your kids watch Dora the Explorer and convincing them that "The Map" is a bona fide interactive GPS device. I'm talking actively teaching reading, writing, arithmetic, and all kinds of science – beginning as soon as they're able to actively listen.

That brings us to the polar opposite of the above situation, the socioeconomically *advantaged*. These are the Stepford Wives who have the education and connections to get a cushy job, but choose not to. They're the perfectly manicured ladies who drive late model minivans, actively solicit mahjongg partners on Facebook, never miss a weekly nail appointment, and have lifetime memberships to some foofy spa. I am fortunate enough to live in a community with several socioeconomically advantaged SAHs who provide an always interesting and entertaining subjective study. Their husbands are typically military consultants or traveling salesmen who hold some sort of privileged middle-management position in corporate America. They have no idea what their wives are up to, and they don't seem to care. Strangely, none of these wives seem to be troubled by this. Don't get me wrong – the stay-at-home moms in my neighborhood possess some laudable skills. I can't think of anyone who's better at cheerleading, social networking, and party planning. We'll get up to three printed flyers in our mailbox, every week for little kid parties or ice cream socials. I have no doubt that these SAHs fully utilize their pricey sheepskins. Workwise, they collectively enjoy brief but vast retail sales experience in upscale boutiques, while a few others were once drug pushers for pharmaceutical reps.

Although these women have the best opportunity to help their children advance, it seems their children tend to spend the most time *away* from mom. The stay-at-homes in my past two upscale neighborhoods seem to be consistently busy with a full schedule of meetings, social activities, sports, and beauty appointments, all while their children are attending some type of boutique daycare. Unfortunately, despite their best efforts, it often leads to failure. By the time these children are in their early teens, they're running buck wild. I have personally observed some of them drinking six-packs on the back of a golf cart, wrecking mailboxes, vandalizing our community center, throwing obnoxious parties while the parents aren't home, and smoking drugs in the park. And all the while mom is too busy doing whatever it is she does to stop them. The things that these little bastards are allowed to do blow my mind. Yet, when confronted, these SAHs vigorously defend their angel children, presumably to protect their own reputations. Privilege does not always lead to privilege, as will be evidenced in a few years from now.

Finally, there are the old-school stay-at-home situations. Although some are a wonderful balance of love and tradition, others stem from an abusive male who may have been raised in an uncommonly strict situation where his father was the king, and his mother wasn't much more than an indentured servant. In these situations, Mom could work, and she probably wouldn't mind working, but Dad forbids it due to his ridiculous old-world or religious beliefs. These men are typically insecure control freaks who believe the world still lives in the 1960s. He is the king of his castle, and will randomly go fishing, boating, golfing, gambling, and to the gentleman's club of his choice, with whomever he wants, whenever he wants – and stay-at-home Mom knows she'd better keep her mouth shut if she wants to continue comfortably doing nothing with her life. Any woman who knowingly accepts such a situation is hopelessly insecure or desperate, and can't possibly provide a positive societal influence for her children. Ironically, her kids would be better off in day care.

Getting past the rampant sarcasm, let's look at the outliers – the successful stay-at-home mom situations.

Some mothers, regardless of socioeconomic status, are conscientious humans and wonderful teachers. I have personally chatted with preschoolers who can speak multiple languages and can name all the components of the cardiovascular system. Some can read earlier than they should, some do math exceptionally well, and others already possess the logic to write fairly complex computer programming code.

There are quite a few organized stay-at-home groups for conscientious mothers, in which children learn how to interact, play chess or a sport, learn an instrument, and other wonderful life skills that will provide them with confidence that will allow them to cast a shadow upon their lesser endowed peers.

There is a very limited window in which you have the opportunity to mold your child into a responsible being who makes smart choices. All children are gifted; it's up to you to embrace and cultivate those gifts. If you have the opportunity to engage in a stay at home situation, do it for the right reasons, and always make the most of it.

And please don't use acronyms. They're so government.

Olivia Black

7: indentured servitude

You can daydream about hanging out with your friends, or sleeping, or eating normally, or exercising, watching a movie, vacationing, enjoying peace and quiet, or anything else you used to have the luxury of doing as a childless person. Your entire existence will be occupied by a selfish, toothless, bald, smelly poopy-pants imp. Ironically, that is exactly the kind of person most parents warned me to avoid.

As a legal parent and guardian, you will be completely responsible for the welfare of your helpless children. No, you cannot ever just leave her in the car, not even for a second. No, you cannot slip out to the store and leave her home alone for "just five minutes." No, you cannot ignore that smelly diaper, his crying, or the need for daily bathing. And no, you certainly cannot rely on prayer, miracles, or God's will to resolve or ignore any sickness or serious medical situation. Avoiding any single basic need, either accidently or purposefully, constitutes neglect or child abuse. The law will take that child away from you and probably put you in jail. And your local news will make sure your reputation as a human being is permanently destroyed well before you've been tried by a jury of your peers. News channels thrive on ratings generated by child neglect stories. So you'd better get into the mindset that you are now that child's cook, butler, maid, servant, nutritionist, health care advocate, education counselor, safety engineer, and cleaning person, and you will be for several years to come. Parenting is not for the selfish.

Begin with childproofing your home as best you can. The best way to be sure things are safe is to empathize with your youngster. Be the brat. Get on your knees and pretend you're three feet tall. You might notice things you can reach that you had never realized could be harmful or even deadly. You'll never forgive yourself for missing them. In some cases, if you missed something and it caused harm, not only would you feel horrible, you could be prosecuted for negligence.

- *Cover your electrical outlets, and remove loose or exposed extension cords.*
- *Do not put heavy items like televisions on narrow or top-heavy stands that could tip over. Children love to climb things.*
- *Tie up, cut off, or modify window blind cords.*
- *Move all the cleaning supplies and knives as high as you can get them.*
- *Add child-safe locks to any cabinets or doors that lead to dangerous products or areas.*
- *Block all stairs with child gates. Remember, children can climb up and fall backwards.*
- *Don't leave hot pans or pots on the stove with their handles facing front.*
- *Anything loose and breakable will be knocked over and broken if it's within baby's reach. Move it or lose it.*
- *Make sure all outside doors are locked.*
- *If you have a swimming pool, ensure you have an approved baby gate.*
- *If you travel in an automobile with your baby, use and app or set an alarm reminding you that child is in the child seat so you won't forget to bring your child with you when you leave the vehicle. It happens.*

- *Eliminate anything loose if it's smaller than a baseball; you would be amazed at what she could put in her mouth and potentially choke on.*

As you navigate the waters of first time parenthood, you'll spend a lot of time shooting countless hours of video that you will never watch documenting all your baby's "firsts." The first gurgle that you'll consider a *word*. The first accidental roll forward that you'll call *crawling*. Enjoy reliving the memory of his first occurrence of *vandalism* as he involuntarily chucks your in-contract smartphone at your 4K smart television, effectively smashing both devices. Great arm!

Fortunately, babies sleep a bunch during their early years, as their tiny bodies exhaust all their energy in the growth process. Unfortunately, you don't get to choose *when* they sleep. The feeding process is constant – it's every few hours while they're tiny. It is not uncommon for your child to wake in the middle of the night, screaming bloody murder, because she is hungry. And no, Miss Convenience – you can't just leave a bottle and some snacks in her crib.

It is important for you to establish that nights are for sleeping and days are for waking. Some children tend to be more active at night. *Experts* advise you to discourage your kids from sleeping during the day, getting them into a more normal routine, at a few months into their lives. This involves letting your baby "cry it out," essentially ignoring her until she cries herself to sleep. There are two schools of thought on this process. Some children are needier than others. There are feeding challenges, cramps, fear, sickness, and other problems they can't communicate to you just yet. Later in life, ignoring your child's needs could create detachment issues, and even underlying trust concerns that could crop up from not being there for your crying child. On the other hand, it is thought that too much coddling could result in a less independent child. The truth is no one is quite sure. We may never know if the *cry it out* method is good or bad for children, but one or the other might make *your* life less miserable.

Me? I caved every time. I couldn't handle more than five minutes of crying that seemed to get worse by the minute. Josh found his son may have been suffering from cramps provided by the peanut proteins in his ex-wife's bottled breast milk, after finding out she was subsisting on a diet of PB and Fluff. When he switched to formula, things improved drastically. Eventually, children learn to sleep on their own. It was a very tough two years with each of mine.

And no, you cannot wait until the morning to change her diaper when you know it needs to be changed. You'll usually smell it quite readily, but other times you will need to check for wetness frequently. And when shit happens, you'll know it. Change that diaper without hesitation, or you'll be dealing with a very upset child when a painful diaper rash sets in. Don't forget the Desitin and butt paste – use them liberally.

Early on in the first year, babies are fairly stationary. You can usually put them down on a floor somewhere, in a safe and child-proofed place, and surround them with pillows or a baby gate. They may roll around a bit, but you shouldn't have to worry about them escaping your house and getting on a bus. My kids stayed strapped in their comfy car seats a bit more than most frilly mothers would approve of. Those seats not only strap into modern baby carriages, but they fit nicely into shopping carts and easily strap on to kitchen chairs. We'd leave our kids in their chairs on the floor next to us when we went out to eat. If we were lucky, they'd stay sleeping. We weren't lucky too often.

And these are the years where everything goes into the mouth. Hands, feet, toys, keys, phones, cords, trash, pets, dirt, and even things that are nailed down. I remember being at a party several years ago and watching a small child grab a beer bottle off a coffee table, immediately putting it into his mouth. Someone pulled it away quickly as it spilled everywhere, but I am fairly sure that child had a sip before he let go. Fortunately, it wasn't some sort of poisonous household cleaner. Things happen very quickly, so keep everything you don't want in his mouth somewhere that he can't possibly reach it.

You'll learn that boys tend to be more mechanical. Before he can talk, your son will quickly figure out how to disable your child-safe locks, learn to disassemble things that engineers have trouble with, and will climb on to surfaces you thought weren't accessible. And he will gaze in wonder as he watches a variety of things (like your keys) magically disappear in that amazing device called a toilet.

At this age, girls are a bit easier to manage. Most will remain slightly more stationary, spending her time learning how to speak and play nicely while developing her mental faculty at a much faster pace than boys.

This is typically Mom's time to shine. The child is still a cute novelty, and she will still be receiving lots of attention and outside help from family and friends. Don't feel guilty about accepting help – the friendly offers won't usually last long. And once they're gone, you're that baby's bitch for years   to   come.

8: toddler fodder

Now that your little angels are mobile, the easy days are over. You can no longer leave them on the floor and assume they'll only move an inch or two as you visit the powder room. During the next few years, at least until they develop their first inkling of common sense at about age 7 or 8, it's a constant and exhausting process to keep them safe.

Josh's daughter was about five when he remarried. At his wedding reception, Josh had to answer questions from the wait-staff and management, be cordial to his guests, and since all his friends were musicians who were also invited guests, Josh was in charge of the entertainment too. Someone pulled Josh aside for a moment as his daughter was talking to one of his guests. He remembered asking the woman if she could keep an eye on his daughter for a moment. It couldn't have been a minute or two later, and when Josh returned, both of them were gone. His heart nearly stopped as he scanned the room for the only three-foot tall person at the party, but she was nowhere to be found. Josh even burst into the ladies' room, looking for her. As Josh was a minute or two into his panic attack, his best buddy walked back into the room, hand in hand with Josh's daughter. Luckily, Josh's buddy was flirting with the front desk chick in the hotel lobby, and he spotted Josh's daughter walking out there alone. Josh knows he was lucky – situations like this have the potential to end badly. Josh didn't let his little girl out of his sight the rest of the night.

Boys, being more physical than girls, will wear you down quickly. Boys will begin exploring everything. They'll climb on anything they can reach. Inexperienced climbers tend to fall, so prepare yourself for a series of bumps and bruises. Fortunately, toddlers tend to be pretty malleable, so a fall that might disable an adult is usually not as big of a deal for a little person. They'll play hide-and-go-seek, sometimes without telling you they're hiding. As a toddler, a formerly wild friend got stuck on a roof, locked himself in a car, fell from the top of monkey bars in a playground (they were on concrete in those days), took a few rocks to the head (which explained many things), and ended up in many other strange situations that he can vaguely remember. He estimates he used up at least seven of his nine lives.

Girls tend to be much more pensive and cerebral at this age. They're more apt to hunker down and play with other girls, dolls, or toys, while developing speech and social skills. Girls are exponentially easier at this age in general.

This is the stage in which potty training becomes a thing. Be prepared to incentivize your child to go potty, as proven by the good folks at Freakonomics. Stock up on M&Ms – they're much cheaper than disposable diapers.

Mealtime will become a chore, as your tiny humans begin to express their displeasure at eating things that are good for them. Mac n' cheese, PBJ (as long as there are no peanut allergies in the household, as there are in ours), pizza rolls, and chicken fingers become staple foods. Get used to preparing two dinners – one for the brat, and one for the rest of the family. Many moms are having success introducing other foods using Pinterest for nouveaux presentation ideas. You'd be amazed at how a smiley face or cartoon made of vegetables suddenly becomes more palatable.

As toddlers, both boys and girls are watching and emulating everything they see, which will influence their personalities as they progress into the next stage of maturity. They'll learn to speak and pick up quite an impressive vocabulary by the age of three. Don't be too concerned if your boy takes a little longer than a girl – they all progress individually, and he'll catch up for sure. They'll learn most of the alphabet and some basic counting from your great teaching or from educational television shows like Sesame Street. Toddlers learn the basics of tone and inflection in speech from your example. This is why it is so critical that you control the environment as best you can at this stage. Avoid exposure to angry situations, foul language, extreme sarcasm, and teenage sitcoms that display disrespectful and sarcastic behavior, even in a so-called humorous manner (I'm looking at you, Disney Channel and Nick). Be cognizant how you act around your family and friends. Be the person you want your child to be. Or at least act that way when your toddlers are awake.

Toys get slightly more complicated and expensive during these years. But don't worry about temper tantrums or disappointing them, because they'll have blurred memories of these years.

These are also the years in which you'll notice developmental disorders. According to the CDC, Autism spectrum disorder (ASD) is a developmental disability that can cause social, communication and behavioral challenges. Kids with ASD may communicate, interact, behave, and learn in ways that are different from most other people. The learning, thinking, and problem-solving abilities of people with ASD can range from gifted to severely challenged. Some people with ASD need a lot of help in their daily lives; others need less.

A diagnosis of ASD now includes several conditions that used to be diagnosed separately, including autistic disorder, pervasive developmental disorder, and Asperger syndrome. People with ASD often have problems with social, emotional, and communication skills. They might repeat certain behaviors and might not want change in their daily activities. Diagnosing ASD can be difficult. Doctors look at the child's behavior and development to make a diagnosis. ASD can sometimes be detected at 18 months or younger. By age 2, a diagnosis by an experienced professional can be considered very reliable. However, many children do not receive a final diagnosis until they're much older. If you're concerned, check with your baby's practitioner.

Bottom line: you'll be exhausted, but they're so freakin' weird and cute that you'll have a lot of laughs. Fortunately, or unfortunately, these years seem to pass quickly. Hopefully, you're young and energetic. Don't let your guard down regarding safety, because they still don't have much common sense. Stock up on energy drinks, or have a stable of babysitters lined up.

9: i hate haiku

I have to laugh at those sappy mothers who cry as they drop their kids off for their first day of kindergarten. They're the same ones who cried when they dropped those same kids at TK1, exactly one year before that. And shed tears at pre-school, before that. And at daycare before that. Kleenex must make a fortune on the first day of school. Why do they cry? Who knows why any woman does anything she does? Personally, I danced like Shakira, did Willy Wonka cartwheels, and sang George Michael's "Freedom" loudly and proudly the moment I'd completed my handoff. The other parents still give me funny looks to this day.

My son came home with an assignment from Language Arts, whatever that is. It sounded like a class on tagging buildings with clever graffiti. He had no idea what he was supposed to do. He's entirely left-brained, which I understand is a valuable trait in today's liberal arts society. He freaked out in frustration, worrying he might get a bad grade, and completely ruined everyone's night. I had to step in to save the world again. After all, that is my job as a parent, next to being a superhero, isn't it? Sadly, I'm a published author, and I didn't have a clue what a Haiku is. I thought he was cursing at me in Spanish. I had to look it up. I thanked my inner-city public education for my lack of knowledge of such an important term.

Haiku (俳句 high-koo) are short poems that use sensory language to capture a feeling or image. They are often inspired by an element of nature, a moment of beauty or a poignant experience. Haiku poetry was originally developed by Japanese poets, and the form was adapted to English and other languages by poets in other countries.

Japanese Haiku traditionally consist of 17 on, or sounds, divided into three phrases: 5 sounds, 7 sounds, and 5 sounds. A seasonal word, called a *kigo*, is typically be added so the reader knows if the story takes place in the summer, fall, winter, or spring.

Mrs. Smith, I'm sorry. I don't know how else to put this, but I couldn't give a shit about your Haiku, and whatever philosophy you might think it may serve sucks. At least traditional poems are tolerable because they rhyme. Shit, even hip-hop is more entertaining than this, and I hate hip-hop. Why are you wasting my child's limited and very valuable learning time with this filler?

Critics agree Haiku were never meant to be translated to Engrish. The Japanese culture, alphabet, and their customs, albeit beautiful and wondrous and whatever, have little to nothing to do with our European and then American bastardization of society. Srsly, have you seen what we've done to sushi? Our school system doesn't have anything else to teach than obscure forms of poetry in these days of The Kardashians, The Chrisleys, and The Robertsons? Who is the idiot who eschewed science, technology, engineering and math and determined that our children might be more globally competitive because he or she can write seventeen syllables of useless bullshit?

Here – I'll give you a few more relevant, and definitely more helpful ideas of things you could be teaching during Haiku time. How about water purification? Nutrition? First aid? Self-defense? How to fix a leak? How to be a responsible and moral citizen? What about delving into the real and potentially selfish or lazy reasons why you are teaching these poor already bored kids to write Haiku? There are countless more useful and meaningful topics you could have spent those five hours preaching. Good luck fixing a flat tire with that Haiku of yours, Mrs. Smith. My left-brain kid couldn't complete your assignment. So I wrote a Haiku for him, complete with a fucking *kigo*:

Wasting my spring night
With this stupid Haiku crap
I could be drinking.

I'm very happy for Basho, Issa, Shiki, Lee Gurga and Jack Kerouac. Thanks so much for creating literary art that makes my child less competitive. Art is wonderful, but save it for those who care for it — and for those who have the means and spare time to enjoy it. The last thing I wanted to do after a tough day at work was learn what a Haiku was, and then write one for my flustered kid.

Elementary school is where your children will learn their basic educational survival skills, including reading and writing the ridiculously complex potpourri of a language called *English*. Never mind that every other civilized country in the world teaches their native language, *as well as English,* at this level. Ironically, American children may not realize there are actually other *countries* until their second or third year of college. I think I was about twelve when I finally learned the entire world didn't speak English and celebrate the Fourth of July. I thought Spanish speakers were just trying to be confusing.

Your child will repeatedly ask you why he has to learn how to spell words correctly. Your reply should be something along the lines of, "So you won't look like a moron when you post comments on Instagram." Oh, wait - Instagram requires *typing*. Kids now use Snapchat, because that's *easier*. There goes that argument.

Children will learn how to count to like a million and develop some basic math skills. Even if you have already taught your child algebra, she will be forced to succumb to the level of the 21 other dummies in her class who weren't quite as fortunate.

It's no secret that American education is a complete disaster. Out-of-touch administrators who have never sat in a classroom wrestle with an apathetic teachers' union, and nothing ever changes as the rest of the world passes our children by at light speed. Older teachers fight change, because they're close to retirement and downright lazy. Parents complain their children has too much homework and it's interfering with soccer practice. Charter and most private schools suffer from the same inertia. If you think home schooling is the answer, wait until you hear your friends' opinion on that. Home schooling was a victim of some clever social engineering, and now is publicly scorned as "damaging to your child's social development."

While I was originally writing this chapter, my sixth grade son was learning what a *delta* and a *coastal plain* are. I've lived no further than 45 minutes from the Atlantic coast my entire life, and I don't ever remember referring to either of those terms in speech or in written communication. When I returned to edit this book six month later, he had completely forgotten what a delta and a coastal plain were. He did correctly guess they had something to do with water.

Poorly written textbooks are distributed by a well-entrenched monopolistic corporate entity. Their authors have predetermined that a sixth-grade student will be a more productive citizen if he learns how to spell mortally obsolete words like *scoundrel, blunder, haughty, dawdle, taut, quintet,* and *tepid.* I was surprised to find that culturally relevant words, such as *merger, acquisition, dividend, collateral, bankruptcy, outsourcing,* and *restructuring* were curiously omitted from his lessons. Maybe I'm less insightful than nerdy Jeopardy-playing bookworms, because I still don't have a single clue what a Haiku is, or what most of their irrelevant textbook teachings will do for my son later in life. I get a step closer to advocating home schooling for any children every day.

Elementary school teachers will also introduce your children to religion-like folklore that will help them sleep at night, including portraying the original American discoverers and pioneers as kind and gentle heroes rather than the skull-crushing conquerors, terrorists, and proponents of biological warfare they truly were. I hate to bash open the piñata of truth, but in reality, Columbus, whose real Italian name was *Colombo*, incidentally, was more of an Italian terrorist. Supposedly, Columbus and the Spaniard soldiers under his command regularly used kidnapping, torture, and mutilation to govern Hispaniola. Today's young soft-minded children are taught the fairytale that Columbus and his fellow sailors gave "Indians" copious high-fives and showered them with gifts.

George Washington most certainly did not chop down that cherry tree. Most likely, he had one or more of the hundreds of *slaves* he *owned* since the age of 11 do it for him. As a matter of fact, if you really want to get angry, then you'll verify that Washington may have been a ginger, and his false teeth were made from either hippopotamus or elephant tusks rather than wood. Better call PETA.

For you few bible-toters who have made it this far, our founding fathers had absolutely no intention of forming the United States as a Christian nation. Jefferson personally and publicly thought Christianity was a ridiculous fairytale.

According to cartoonish historians, Pocahontas and John Smith may have been "friends," but that "friendship" would have placed Smith on the sexual predator watch list in today's world. She is thought to have been 12 in 1607 when she and old-man Smith supposedly swapped spit.

And old Benny Franklin wasn't stupid enough to fly a kite with a key attached to it during a lightning storm. He was too busy womanizing.

I won't go on.

I have to wonder if teachers actually believe the nonsense they teach. If you want an alternative, non-fictional perspective on American history, begin with Howard Zinn's *A People's History of the United States: 1492 to Present*. I recommend you re-up your prescription for sleeping pills before you read that book. I couldn't sleep for a month.

Don't be afraid to ask your children what they learned, and correct them where appropriate. You obviously don't have to tell them the truth about Pocahontas for a few more years, but ensure that your children are not afraid to ask their teachers thought-provoking questions.

Be assured that children in this age group are still soaking up data like sponges. Their brains are on auto-pilot. Although you may not think what you do and what you say matter, your behavior is definitely setting neural patterns in your child's mind, under their "approved behavior" section. That includes cursing, drinking, misbehaving, cougaring, cheating, lying, stealing, and husband beating. If you have a natural tendency to be bad, hide that from your child as best you can. They're watching and listening to everything you do whether you think so or not. Voices carry.

Mild bullying will begin to present itself, as early as second grade. More assertive children won't find themselves victimized. Teach them to stand up for themselves early, and they'll be fine. More on bullying later.

Some children grow faster than others, and that's completely normal. It's not unusual to see a six-footer with a cheesy moustache in fifth grade sitting next to his four-foot best friend who still has a baby nose. Same goes for maturity. Someone playing nicely with Lego one month might suddenly decide he is done with toys and be sexting girls the next month. It can happen that quickly.

My son had to have *purple* sneakers. I warned him that his friends might say they were "chick sneaks," but he didn't care. He has a pretty strong personality, so I thought he could handle the nonsense. I let him make the purchase with his own money. Two weeks later, he decided he was never going to wear purple sneakers again. Things change quickly in elementary school. He moved on to lime green, which is apparently a much more acceptable color.

Towards the end of elementary school, your children will begin to develop their preliminary social skills, and will probably introduce you to their first real "best friends." This is where you'll begin to see the first major influence from outside peers. Your son or daughter may begin to say things or behave in a manner that may be inconsistent with anything you've observed before. If it is behavior that doesn't agree with your principals, you'd better nip it in the bud, because it's only going to get worse.

The most important fact about the elementary school years is that you, your community, your family, their teachers, their friends, and their friends' parents are collectively building an irreparable foundation for your child's future character. His or her mind is being molded into what will ultimately become their adult self. You won't always be in control of this molding process. Take little

Alex for example. When Alex was in sixth grade, he started hanging out with another sixth grader named Tyler who had just moved in to his recently dilapidated neighborhood. Tyler's father was a fledgling know-it-all salesman at some industrial company. Apparently, Tyler's dad was proud of the fact that he was making a six-figure salary with no college degree. "I'm not going to push Tyler to go to college if he doesn't want to. I didn't go, and I'm doing alright."

BAM. You'd think Alex's dad just found out Tyler may have Ebola. I can still see vapor trails from Alex's dad's pulling Alex away from Tyler and his father's terrible advice. Alex's father sold his house and moved to another school district. I'm sure you agree that it's not a good plan to tell an eleven-year-old child that it's cool to limit his goals based on the fact that daddy happened to luck out and land a cushy sales job. Be involved in your child's life, *and* in the lives of your child's friends. If you don't know the influences your child is being exposed to, you can't save him from the bad ones.

Of course, you can't always have insight into everything that's influencing your child. Many "gamers" chat online with other kids from all over the world. Most of the kids are probably alright, since it is unlikely they'll ever physically meet or physically interact with your child. But, as in any other situation, there are quite a few who aren't headed in the right direction. When our 11-year-old son began chatting with deep-voiced men on his Team Speak account, I began to get worried. He says they were only 14 or so, but how the hell would he know? I decided it was time to run interference. I had to pull the plug on the internet at 9 PM. Blamed it on a constant denial of service attack that one of his supposed *friends* initiated. We've allowed him progressively later bedtimes since then along with a little more freedom, but we monitor his conversations periodically, and we too chat with his online friends to let them know we may be listening. There's no way to hear or know everything, but we're confident our child has his head screwed on pretty straight.

This is a good time to remind kids that they're being watched. No, not to get them paranoid, but to make them cognizant that their grades, their behavior, and their activities will soon begin to matter. In just a few short years, colleges will begin to evaluate your children and their activities. Getting into the right school can make a huge difference in their career and the subsequent opportunities they are offered. You, as a parent, need to let them know that it is ultimately your child's responsibility to get good grades and do the right thing, unless they plan to live under a bridge when you boot them out of your home at age 18. A little well-placed fear never hurt anyone. Plant the seeds while you still can.

Remember, elementary school kids are just that — *elementary*. They're young, inexperienced, and extremely gullible. You'll need to keep your eyes and ears open, to ensure they're not heading down the wrong path with the wrong people.

Once unacceptable behavior becomes tolerated, it becomes cemented, and then it's insanely difficult to break. At this age, there is no good reason to let anything slide. If you do, they'll drive you crazy as they attempt to push their limits. This is the first time your kid might act angry that you're "ruining his or her life," but so what? Most kids 12 and under are incapable of holding grudges for more than a day. Do it now, because re-aligning your child in middle school gets much more difficult. They subconsciously want to be disciplined and controlled because it makes them feel safe.

One more note, especially about elementary school *boys*. Once they hit about 11 or 12, they'll start to flex their muscles and push your buttons. For a good solid year, your youngster will question you and your judgment. He'll ask you why he needs to go to bed at 8 PM, and then defy you to see what happens. He'll suddenly become a mean little punk and make you miserable while shopping, dining out, visiting friends, vacationing, and all the other great family bonding activities you fondly remember enjoying just a year ago. Before you call in a priest for an exorcism, know this is only a phase. Be strong, be firm, and remember it goes away in a year or less.

Don't worry – your little girls will continue to be little angels, at least through the end of sixth grade. Sybil won't arrive until the middle of seventh.

10: mid-school life crisis

Here's where things begin to get sketchy. Ever wonder why they call it *middle* school? It may just be because this is where they'll learn how to use that particular finger. Don't be surprised to see it pointed in your direction (usually behind your back).

Seventh grade is when little kids suddenly think they're big. They'll tell you they no longer need babysitters – but they definitely do. They'll tell you they're not into the opposite sex – but they unquestionably are. They'll swear up and down that they didn't do whatever malfeasance you're blaming on them – but they most certainly did. Trust me, this age sucks more than any other. Unsupervised children tend to do more stupid things during this age than at any other time in their life. This is your last chance to get any truth out of these conniving little bastards. Fortunately for parents, at this age most children are still inexperienced liars.

Clothing will begin to become a large expense, especially with girls, as they're actively trying to copy their heroes on their favorite reality show. If you've managed to keep them away from those senseless shows, you may be able to postpone this expense, but only until the peer pressure catches on. Your cheap trips to Target, Kohl's, and Children's Place will be replaced with trips to Hollister and Abercrombe, where you'll find yourself buying the exact same clothing at five times the price. Don't forget the mandatory Starbucks trip while at the mall, which will set you back another twenty bucks. Boys are usually a bit more tolerable and affordable at this age, unless they're leaning gay.

Your child's gaming system or portable electronic devices will replace you as their constant companion. The bedroom they've avoided for years will become their new hideout. Any bunk beds (and all the other really cool kids' stuff you carefully chose and they've loved for years) will suddenly become childish and annoying in their eyes, so be prepared to at least get a new bedspread.

Any voluntary help you used to get around the house suddenly becomes a painful chore and ceases to be offered. Any company you used to have while shopping or running errands is now a march of inexcusable embarrassment, because regardless of how hot you still are, you've somehow morphed into an ugly old troll in their eyes. As depressing as it sounds, the truth is that you'll be reduced from a constant loving companion to nothing more than an offensive, nagging, bitchy automatic teller machine. Get used to that for at least the next six years.

My daughter returned home from some bullshit leisure time activity to find me sweaty and exhausted doing yard work. An energetic young soul helping us with the yard would have been a blessing. But this never crossed her mind, not even for a millisecond. The only attention you'll ever get after age 12 is an obligatory token hug, and only when you've given her 20 bucks for snacks. Or, if she's sick, she'll suddenly become your best friend, but only if you cater to her every whim. I can't count how many times I've wished I could trade my selfish teens in for their younger selves.

In the olden days, kids would leave home around 13 or 14 and begin families of their own. Funny, right? Actually, if you consider the entire time frame of humanity's existence as 24 hours, we've only decided to keep middle schoolers home for about six minutes. It's unfortunately natural for these little turds to begin spreading their wings and wanting a taste of independence.

Young teens are developing their own cute little opinions, typically as wrong and obnoxious as can be. Their lives are beginning to get less cartoonish and more serious. This is the age at which you could lose control of your children, if you don't instill strong moral values and discipline of some sort. This is the most critical time for you to be actively involved in their lives. Kids running around without supervision, at this age, are dangerous. Lose them now, and you may never get them back.

You've got to decide what you're going to do about curfews, who they hang out with, and where they're allowed to go. They'll begin to push their boundaries to see just how far you'll bend. Of course, you have the best intentions. But 13-14 years of wiping their butts gets old. You'll often flirt with the idea of letting them do whatever the hell they want, just to get them out of your hair. But persevere – you need to.

Linda had two sons. I knew her while she was thriving in her career as a real estate salesperson, ultimately becoming the manager of her local office. As a divorced mother, her success gave her the affirmation she had failed to receive from her marriage. Linda figured her boys were now in their early teens, and they were old enough to look after themselves. I told her this would be a bad idea, but she blew me off.

Linda worked late into the evenings and was rarely home. What Linda didn't realize was that her boys had been hanging around with another unsupervised crew, and her home had become the party spot. Kids will be kids, and kids without limits will undoubtedly go wild. They'd throw wild parties at her house whenever she went away for the weekend, and it wasn't uncommon for the police to be called to break things up. Linda blew it off, still thinking this was "normal." Her sons got into all kinds of legal trouble, during middle and high school.

Eventually two of her sons finished high school, and one became a prominent drug dealing felon and crack addict. The other is a disastrous welfare wreck with two illegitimate children and has been jailed for not paying child support. To this day, Linda is completely oblivious to the fact that her selfish negligence during the middle school years most likely ruined her children's lives.

If I could give you one piece of advice, which might just save your child during middle and high school, it would be to get your kids involved with a music program. Administrators typically won't run up to your kid and say, "Hey, Balthazar, I think you'd be great at the trumpet! Come join me in this wonderful music program, right now!" Band is one of those quirky things that might be mentioned in a small obscure blurb on the school flyer – the one you were probably quick to ignore and recycle. You, as a parent, will need to choose the right electives, or approach the administration and ask that your child be included in music schools or band. *This begins in middle school.*

Band kids tend to form a cohesive little clique. Teenage wind ensembles and string musicians are kind of nerdy for the most part, and that's a good thing. Personally, I'd rather have my kid hanging out with nerds, who will most likely end up on the right side of society.

Later, in high school, they'll naturally progress to a much larger clique. Our local high school has one of the largest bands in our state. Close to ten percent of the student body is in their band. Our daughter walked into high school as a freshman already knowing over two hundred kids. She never felt awkward or insecure, and she seems so much happier than she did pre-music. Band gives her security and a purpose. Music was the best thing that has ever happened to her.

Recent studies show that musically inclined children have an easier time studying, and they tend to achieve better academic success. Performing music is basically a combination of subliminal math and logic.

High school comes around quickly. This is the time when your child's grades, test scores, and activities truly begin to matter, because colleges will begin paying attention. Kids generally aren't too worried about anything during middle school. Life is still on autopilot. It's your job to make them very aware that they'll need to take the controls and teach them to fly as best as they can.

Set them straight, once again, during the summer before high school. Let them know how important it is to do well over the next four years, because this will give them *choices* in the future. If they want that one-acre house and the happy family that comes with it, they're going to need to earn it.

11: high school drama

Yes, the organized activities you choose to participate in during high school are important. Yes, your grades absolutely do matter. Yes, your SAT and ACT test scores *are* relevant. And yes, you little shit – you *are* going to college, whether you want to or not. Why? Because I'll be damned if you think you're going to end up living on my couch, eating my food and jerking off into my towels in your mid-30s.

The high school bubble will be your child's first experience in dealing with society. Relationships will be tested, judgment will be tried, and your child will begin to define who they're going to be for the rest of their lives. This is your absolute last chance, as a parent, to have any influence on your children.

Although high school seems so incredibly earth-shatteringly important while you're there, once you're out of that bubble, you get a clean slate. Unless you're an all-star athlete, nothing you did, or achieved, or learned in high school will really make one iota of difference in your later life. Although kids don't realize this until much later, a social status as a hero, geek, star, or loser, will be completely erased by the time you're twenty. If kids realized this during high school, imagine how pleasant learning could be. But at the time, status is *everything*. It seems eternal, and you'll never be able to convince most hormonal high school children otherwise. Growing up this free comes with ridiculous pressure and consequences.

As they progress from freshman to senior, you may begin to find your children overly concerned with one word – *party*. *Everyone* seems to be having a party, every day of the year. And you supposedly have to let them go, because, and I quote, *"everyone will be there." Everyone* is *always* there. This is why you'll need to be in tune with your child and his or her circle of friends, so you can verify that there really is a party, that it will be supervised by a team of responsible adults, and that *everyone* is indeed attending.

Please don't ever tell your children this, but honestly, with today's ridiculously outdated curriculum, underpaid teachers, programmatic budget cuts, and ridiculously gilded varsity football merriments, more than half of your child's high school experience is largely a waste of time. I would venture to speculate that by the time you have graduated from eighth grade, you should have mastered all the basic reading, writing, science, and mathematics skills an average person employed in more than 50% of typical American jobs (retail, government, services, various trades, driving) will ever need to function in society. Most work skills are learned in trade schools or post-graduate programs, or more so, on the job, and do not require mastery of most high school subject matter.

Does that mean most workers are dumb? Not necessarily. We force a lot of valuable knowledge in a child's head through eighth grade. But honestly, when's the last time you used Greek mythology to solve a logistics problem, manually calculated a derivative while installing a window, or needed to know the tenure of William Henry Harrison in order to get the mail delivered on time? Granted, knowledge is a wonderful thing. But honestly, how many of these facts do you personally recall and use in day to day activities? Even the most successful and tenured adults would readily fail any of the tests we passed during high school.

An article in The Washington Post explained that many students participating in the 2013 White House Science

Fair said that they created their projects outside of school by teaching themselves the science involved or seeking out mentors in the community and at universities. Easton LaChapelle, 17, of Mancos, Colorado, taught himself enough computer coding and electronic skills to build a prosthetic arm controlled by brain waves for about $400. Easton got his inspiration when he met a girl with an $80,000 prosthetic arm at a science and engineering festival. "I'm all self-taught," he said, explaining that his high school lacks the science courses and equipment to help him work at the level necessary for his project. "School is basically a waste of time. I'd be better off with those seven hours if I could just use them working on my own." Obviously, this won't work for every student. But it might work for many. It would have worked for me.

So what are we teaching kids in high school? Current public and private educators seem to think that homecoming décor, the theme of this year's prom, the win-loss record of the varsity football team, or knowing the intent of J.D. Salinger's while writing *The Catcher in the Rye* is more important than CPR, how to write programming code, how to grow food, how to balance a checkbook, how to address an envelope, how to fix a broken *anything*, or any other skill a student would find useful in life or today's workplace. Rather than allow students to choose an elective curriculum based on their inherent skills or interests, our school administrators think it's better to just shove lots of things they'll readily forget – including English literature, world history, and calculus – down their throats and have them reluctantly regurgitate this information via short-term memory. In many schools, especially in lower socio-economic areas, teachers will push their students through to the next grade, regardless of whether they've actually learned anything. It's not uncommon to find high school graduates with C averages who legitimately cannot read or write.

Most high schools are a complete failure. We either can't afford to fix them, or no one sees the need to do so. The former used to be considered a slightly more valid excuse, until Facebook's Mark Zuckerberg tried to rescue Newark's school system with a generous $100 million donation back in 2010. Apparently, a whole bunch of rich folks got a little more rich, yet five years later, Newark's test scores were actually worse. Could Newark's schools have achieved greatness with Zuckerberg's gift? Perhaps, if humans weren't responsible for deciding where the money was spent. Ultimately, it remains your job, as a parent, to fill in the missing blanks and ensure your children learn all they'll need to know to become a successful adult. Remember that you will always be your child's primary teacher.

Here's the twist. Our education system is what it is, and it won't change anytime soon. High school, no matter how much of a waste of time it is, is not optional. You can't ever agree that it is a waste of time, or you'll permanently damage your child's perspective. You must convey how important it is for your children to take grades nine through twelve dead seriously and do the absolute best they can, because in most cases, it is absolutely critical to the success of their future.

College Admissions have turned from an objective scores-based policy into a circus of popularity. Sports, primarily football and basketball, are more popular than ever. The better your sports team, the more applicants a college will receive, and the more selective that school can become. Popular colleges no longer look solely for straight

A's and high SAT scores. Today, you practically need a resume with sports, activities, thousands of volunteer hours, real work experience, mission trips, math clubs, scientific breakthroughs, a cure for cancer, and three more pages of fluff that makes you look like the biggest potential success that school has ever admitted.

Why are colleges so choosy? *Marketing.* Over the years, colleges have learned to identify people who succeed not purely as academics, but also as people who appear to work well with others. The more success stories the college can brag about, the more they can charge for admission and merchandise, the more donations they're apt to receive in the future, and the more selective they can be with regard to admissions. The most ridiculous offender has got to be The University of Florida, especially during the Tim Tebow era in which the Florida Gators were the college football team of the universe. At one point, this state college was looking for students with a 4.4 GPA, practically unobtainable ACT/SAT scores somewhere in the stratosphere, plus an unlikely and improbable social schedule that would make even the POTUS seem stretched. All this is required just so you can wear those horribly clashing school colors of orange and blue.

Knowing that getting into the right college is a critical key to success, how do you plant the seeds in the mind of a high school kid who is living in the moment and couldn't give a crap about the future? From experience, I can tell you it's not easy. The best thing you can do is mask your efforts by getting your child accustomed to being involved with as many opportunities for social interaction as possible. Check out scouts, school bands, school and regional sports teams, community service projects, student government, church socials, and other worthwhile opportunities. If your time is limited, or your child is more of an introvert, there are some pretty cool video game opportunities that offer social interaction and some project management experience. There are even lucrative business opportunities for video production people or kids who are good with computers. Embrace their activities, and let them know you're proud of their accomplishments. Their roots will grow deep, and your children will be on the road to becoming content, confident, competent, and successful adults.

If your kid has college aspirations, it's up to you, the parent, to ensure that this college-preparation happens from day zero in high school. I had no idea that there was any high school activity that our child could take part in before the first day of school. But our kid had been jockeying for position by attending high school band auditions before she graduated from middle school. That was crazy smart.

At various junctures, mostly when dealing with a negative social aspect, I've found it important to reinforce the following concepts:

- *Remind kids that there are bosses and there are employees. Smarter kids usually end up as bosses, and bosses usually make more money.*
- *Remind kids that although their friends are their whole life right now, they'll probably never see most of their classmates again after they graduate. High school pals last for four short years, but they typically aren't around for the next seventy.*

I would be careless if I failed to issue the following warning about your children and their mental state during their high school years. Even if you survived a vicious post-partum change, you will still be ill-prepared to meet your child's newly evil, narcissistic, and often sociopathic alter-ego, who will unfailingly present him or herself right about the time that he or she hits tenth grade.

Melinda was a girl who was the warmest, kindest, most caring and considerate teenager on the planet. Completely dedicated to her studies and demonstrating sound moral judgment, I was convinced this girl was on the right track and going places in life. She shied away from boys and parties and all the other silly nonsense her status-quo friends were involved in. Then, one day, in tenth grade, she must have discovered she had a vagina. Her entire disposition changed, seemingly overnight. She began to worry about what boys thought about her hair and her clothes. She decided it wasn't cool to hang out with her parents – or talk to any adult, for that matter. She became distant and apparently had developed some kind of secret agenda. From that moment forward, she became an entirely different person. Her parents wouldn't say Melinda was the most difficult lying and scheming little bitch in the Western Hemisphere, but by the time she was a senior and turned 18, she was in the running. School was no longer important to her; Melinda's boyfriend was now her priority. All the college tours she took and all her wonderful college preparations and aspirations were cast to the wind as she chose a lackluster local college – ostensibly because her boyfriend went there. She no longer felt it necessary to study for Advanced Placement tests, because she now felt she "didn't need to *rush* her college *experience*," a quote I happened to hear mentioned by a certain boyfriend's idiot mother on several occasions.

Nothing her parents said to her, despite their best intentions and warnings, mattered in the least. She became an entirely different person almost overnight, and there seemed to be no derailing her from her newly misguided track.

Children today mistakenly assume college is a four-year extension of high school. But since they're *so mature* now, they feel there is no need for supervision. Before Melinda graduated high school, she informed her parents she would gladly let them pay for a dorm, and in the same breath, proudly announced she would probably be staying with her boyfriend more than 50% of the time anyway. Her mother almost cried as suffered massive guilt wondering where she could have gone wrong.

Be prepared for the high school electrical short, and try not to take it personally. Young minds have so many outside influences that are beyond your control. All you can do is provide a solid foundation while you still have the power, provide a safe haven when they crash, and hope for the best.

One of the valedictorians made an impressive speech on my daughter's graduation day that displayed solid maturity and truth. The speaker said something to the effect of, "Whatever you did or whoever you were during the past four years doesn't matter. It's over. Your real life begins today." The stadium was silent. You could practically hear all these graduates simultaneously thinking, "Man, this shit just got real." The valedictorian mostly right – nothing really mattered, except the grades and test scores you achieved and how well you prepared for college admissions.

People change. We all do. But if you're interested in building a solid foundation for your children, be aware that your parental influence will wane significantly during those high school years. Build your foundation as early as you can, and build solidly. Remember that high school kids are just that – *kids*. Don't buy in to the silly notion that they're *young adults*, because they are certainly not *adults* in any sense of the word. Do not be afraid to exercise sound authority and discipline for fear of being disliked. It's a long and uncomfortable time to wait, but they'll thank you in twenty years. You'll see.

The smartest thing you can do as a parent of a high school student is convince your kid to enroll in "dual enrollment." Many high schools offer programs in conjunction with local community or four-year colleges in which you can earn real college credits during high school. *And it's free.* Several students graduate high school with a two-year associates' degree, and are able to enter college at just under the third-year level. That achieves two very worthy things: it shaves nearly half the tuition costs from your child's student loan, and it's usually easier to get accepted to any school as a second or third year student due to attrition in enrollment. Even the Gator Nation admits that fact.

You could also go the Advanced Placement (AP) route, which means your child would take advanced "college level" courses that are supposed to prepare him or her for some insanely difficult end-of-year test. If your child scores at least a 3 on a scale of 5, some colleges will award them college credit for that test. Some schools require a 4 or 5; and other schools may not accept your AP score as a college credit. Colleges are quite finicky with regards to AP credits. Some prestigious colleges have stopped giving academic credit for AP tests scores. Brown, Dartmouth, and some Columbia departments do not offer any academic credit for even the highest AP scores, indicating the notion that "A Dartmouth education should occur at Dartmouth. Tea anyone?"

There is a downside for educationally advanced kids, which I selfishly considered a bonus in the long-term. An 18-year-old junior won't have the time to waste palling around with other naïve 18 year-old freshmen, effectively eliminating at least part of the unnecessary social drama. And your 18 year-old may not be old enough to get into the bars his classmates will be hanging out at. Maybe the social confusion will induce studying instead of *twerking*.

Sports in high school are held with great importance, and will forever eclipse the attention given to any academic achievements in most schools. Our local high school football team made it to the regional finals, and everyone in the neighborhood seems to be celebrating. I'm all about watching a great game. But here's the problem.

The same school's female soccer and golf teams both had stellar years, but we didn't hear much more than a peep about them. The swim team too has been rocking the record books. And their marching band continually places well in regional competitions. But does the principal invite the entire school to line up and send any of those groups off when they attend competitions? Nope. Is there a pep rally held before the math team heads off to meet their arch enemy? Nope. Is anyone or anything else lauded the way a group of boys who play a sport that involves more physical contact and head injuries than most? Absolutely not.

And talk about perks? Whether you admit it or not, you know football players on the high school and collegiate levels get free tutor assistance, early and excused dismissals, celebrity status at local restaurants and businesses, and there's even talk about compensating amateur college athletes with salaries and sponsorships.

How is this fair? It's not. So why do we stand for it? Because no one has ever dared to make a fuss about America's pastime - *football*. Baseball used to be the American thing, but admit it, that hasn't been the case in a decade or two. Surprisingly, not even feminists have the balls to talk about this. But fairness isn't the issue. It's the deviation from education which is the real problem.

For schools to begin to change and succeed, we need to remove sports. Sure, there are lessons in collaboration, teamwork, and physical activity. But these are lessons better taught by parents, or community or private organizations, rather than establishments with a primary function of educating children. It's time to pull sports out of schools. Let's celebrate academics for a change if we want our children and country to be competitive globally. A few outstanding football players isn't going to do dick for the good ol' USA.

School was created to educate our children in an effort to prepare them for the workplace. It does a terrible job preparing children for *life* because the curriculum is a disastrous collection of century-old methods protected by powerful teacher and textbook lobbies. My children graduated high school with good grades without knowing how to write a check, address an envelope, create a resume, or perform CPR. But nowhere in the original plans to create local schoolhouses did anyone envision the most important part of schooling might be sports.

So what happened to Melinda? She enjoyed her college experience a little too much. She dropped out early in her second year, depressed after a devastating break-up when her high school boyfriend, the man she planned to marry and have children with, decided he enjoyed the intimate company of men a little more than women. She still lives off-campus with a few boys who are still enrolled, and enjoys the college experience of others while earning poverty-level wages at a local retail store.

12: summer slide

Now that I've pissed off religious types, sports fans, and virtually half of all Americans by telling the truth, let's now attack conservatives. I dare you to walk into any public place in America and yell "I'm a Socialist, and I'm proud of it." You won't. Why not? You'd be labelled as a heretic because the super-wealthy folks who control our government through campaign bribes – I meant *contributions* – and mass media via shareholder voting have made socialism a dirty word. Ironically, your police force is Socialism at work. Firefighters and trashmen? Socialism. Veterans Administration hospitals? Your Post Offices, weather centers, parks, libraries, military, prisons, highways, and even your public education system – all bottom-line textbook *socialist*. As a matter of fact, anything your taxes pay for is technically socialist. All of a sudden, this socialism thing doesn't seem as bad as the media wants you to believe it is, does it? I don't recall anyone even broaching this topic in my multi-thousand dollar partially socialized college experience. And why should they? No one ever said college topics had to be *useful,* only *profitable.* I actually learned more about Italian architecture than about American social policy in college.

Critics of socialism are always quick to note that our education system sucks *because* it is socialist. But it doesn't have to suck. And it shouldn't suck. It sucks because we're too *lazy* to fix it. It sucks because teachers' unions don't *want* to change anything. The first change we need is to eliminate that ridiculous two-and-a-half-month summer vacation.

The origin of the two to three-month American summer vacation for school students is strangely vague. Old wives' tales explain that this time was needed to tend to family farms and harvest crops, but harvest time typically isn't until late fall. A more likely scenario was sweltering classrooms, filled with students who couldn't concentrate, and teachers and administrators who would rather be dipping their feet into a bacteria-infested muddy river until the heat subsided. Like Daylight Savings Time, regardless of its origin, it is now outdated, inconvenient, and unnecessary. It's also penalizing me, you, our children, and America's future. One thing is for certain – that all-powerful Socialist teachers' union lobby will ensure that your teachers keep that paid two-month sabbatical until the end of time.

The fundamental question is, does any child, or teacher, really require two months off? I personally can't think of a larger waste of time and talent. That's a whopping 1/6th or nearly 17% of an entire year, in which most children are doing absolutely nothing constructive. More liberal proponents will counter with "Oh, there are things kids learn in the summer." Most won't learn a single useful thing. Their brains turn to mush as they watch re-runs of smart-assed unsupervised teenagers, wealthy no-talent celebrity families, or millionaire hillbillies.

Psychologically, there is a phenomenon loosely called the "Summer Slide," in which students forget up to three months' worth of what they had last learned. Teachers are forced to waste several weeks of the subsequent semester refreshing students to get them up to speed and ready for the new material.

To my dismay, much of the rest of the developed world has also emulated this model. However, the rest of the world's students seem to be excelling at science, technology, engineering and math, while, ironically, only our American students are falling behind.

Do not let your child waste these two months. I know, you're busy working. But it's your turn to teach. Here's a bunch of things you can do with your kids, or hire someone else to do, during those lazy, hazy, crazy days of summer.

- *Music lessons, band camp*
- *Science labs, projects*
- *Environmental studies, projects*
- *Animal studies, farming, shelters*
- *Magic lessons, balloon sculptures*
- *Acting classes, plays*
- *Computer programming, coding, white-hat hacking training*
- *Reading and writing tutors*
- *Internships at parents' workplaces*
- *Volunteer or community service projects*
- *Sports camps*
- *Art, painting, or photography classes*
- *Summer jobs, babysitting, housework*

Maybe, your kids might actually learn the meaning of the word *Socialism* in the summer. Because they sure as hell won't learn it in school.

13: twerking n' jerking

Our then 14-year-old daughter came home crying from her school's sanctioned homecoming dance. She has decided to skip it this year unless something is done to make these dances less pornographic.

Homecoming, like many antiquated events we seem to accept and celebrate without question, is the tradition of welcoming back alumni. Homecoming typically includes various activities for students and alumni, which in most cases is limited to a football game and a drink special at a local haunt. Most high schools host a special homecoming dance in the autumn. Ironically, no one is really coming home to attend this dance, since alumni is typically prohibited from attending.

Knowing darn well what adolescent children are capable of during these largely unsupervised events, I attempted to circumnavigate the question in advance with an alternative family outing at exactly the same time the homecoming dance was scheduled to occur. However, something came up and my plan was foiled. Our daughter begged and pleaded to go to her school's homecoming dance. That elusive yet uber-popular group known collectively as *everyone* was going, which from my count, was a grand total of four. I supposed the stigma of being the only friend who did not go to homecoming might prove to be ruinous. Nonetheless, her grades were excellent and she is typically a very well behaved child, so I caved.

There is a considerable financial investment involved in these school dances. By the time you splurge for a dress, matching shoes (that are worn for roughly five minutes then cast away in a corner), tickets, and of course, a hair stylist and obligatory mani-pedi, you could spend well over the full price of a new iPhone, which is a much better investment in my opinion. We added to the family's revolving debt load and followed the flock. Although she tried on a few dresses that were a bit too revealing, she opted for a more traditional dress that fell well below her knees.

Homecoming night came. Our local school rents a larger facility that can handle the large turnout. I perused the crowd as we searched for a parking spot. Apparently, much has changed since the days of my homecoming dances. Now, we're fairly open-minded folks. But some of these girls were wearing dresses that were so short they might be considered *hooch* (obscene). My momma would not have let me out of the house with a dress like those. We questioned the sanity and judgment of some of the parents who were dropping their scantily-dressed babies off at the curb. We walked our daughter up to the door. She found her crowd, gave me a hug, and ran off giggling. We went home.

A few hours later, we got a phone call. "Mom, can you come get me?" She sounded distressed. We arrived to find her standing outside, alone, and in tears. We went to a diner and had a long chat about what happened.

First of all, any high school dance must have active chaperones. A chaperone's function is to ensure the safety and orderly behavior of the participants. According to our daughter's account, no one seemed to intervene in anything, regardless of what they saw on the dance floor.

Secondly, the young DJ opted to play the uncensored versions of the awful hip-hop songs all her classmates were into. She had never heard these versions, since we monitor what she downloads. There is a reason why music is labelled "offensive lyrics." When you're grown, you can listen to an infant banging pans together overlaid with some idiot spewing poorly written poetic profanities if you like. But give kids a chance to develop a choice.

Finally, the latest trend in dancing is something known as "grinding." As a former DJ, Jake can attest that it's been around for a few decades. For the uninitiated, a boy takes his place behind a girl, with or without her permission, and puts his hands on her pelvic area. He then pulls her derriere directly to the front of his reproductive area, physically rubbing on her backside with a youthful vigor to the beat of the awful rap song that's currently playing. Let that image settle in for a moment.

I am not looking to make my hometown anything like Elmore City, Oklahoma. I'm all about children learning to explore the real world and becoming well-informed adults. It's a mess out there, and if you shelter them too much, the culture shock could result in a devastating bout of depression. As a civilization, we need to establish some ground rules. The following common-sense suggestions may help.

If anyone is in attendance who is under the age of 18, which is *always*, ask the school to curb the lyrics. Radio versions of all the popular hip-hop songs are readily available on CDs, iTunes and at Amazon. It's the same stupid song with the same lousy drum machine. Fill in your own profanities if you choose.

Dresses that are too short are inviting the attention of the wrong crowd. Free-spirited mothers need to recalibrate your judgment unless you want to be premature grandparents. Think about this, Mom — that $250,000 it costs to raise a child today will most likely fall upon you.

The "grinding" thing is the main challenge. Since there is inappropriate physical contact with a child, the practice of grinding is technically sexual assault in most jurisdictions, and can be prosecuted by the state attorney whether or not you or your child files charges. The last thing you want to do is wrangle in court over this type of case with an expensive attorney during a very public trial. News headlines will read "Sexual Assault" with "grinding" buried way beneath the fold. School administrators and chaperones may also be named in the suit.

Do you know where the word "Prom" comes from? It's actually an acronym that stands for *Poor Revelation of Maturity*. Well… it really comes from the word *Promenade*. I've always thought my clever acronym fits better. The Promenade fiasco began sometime in the 19th century, as a method for wealthy college boys and girls to meet and mingle. Somehow, it has migrated downwards, age and income-wise, as all silly trends do, probably as a result of some horribly misguided wannabe debutante. Isn't that how all traditions begin?

It's not the dance, or the party, the boy, or the dress that's the exciting part of going to a prom, you foolish uniformed parents. It's a well-known secret that, if you've done your job and she hasn't already blown it during unsupervised middle school sleepovers, it is considered perfectly acceptable (and often expected) for a woman to lose her virginity on prom night. Silly little teenage girls have this dream of their first time being "special." I'm still not sure what is so extraordinary about hundreds of sweaty and obnoxious hormonal teenagers, offensive rap music, twerking, grinding, and the backseat of a car that make prom night so *special*.

Like sports, proms have absolutely nothing to do with education and should not be sponsored by any public or private school. The entire prom debacle causes a tremendous amount of emotional and financial strain for many students and their parents. It's nothing more than another harmful distraction that wastes a tremendous amount of time and consequently damages the education system in the United States. When you think about it, the entire prom process is another socially engineered, profit-motivated trick that causes undue stress, worry, and peer pressure. Here's what you, as a proud prom parent, will be expected to shell out so that your kid can go booty shaking:

- *Prom tickets, up to $200*
- *Dress, up to $400*
- *Shoes, up to $200*
- *Hairdresser, up to $100*
- *Flowers, up to $75*
- *Fancy pre-prom dinner, up to $100*
- *After-prom breakfast, up to $25*
- *Limousine, up to $800*
- *Professional photographs, up to $300*

No matter what your children tell you, it is NOT okay to let your son or daughter spend the night at someone else's house on prom night. No matter what anyone says, the typical prom party host is a single 30-something bimbo mother who swears her 16-year-old angel won't make the same mistake she made 16 years ago. Unfortunately, that doesn't mean she won't leave the door open for *your* child's misfortune, because that's not really Bimbo's problem. Remember your own childhood, and please don't make the mistake of thinking, for one second, that hormones aren't more powerful than words, muscles, or even bullets. Teens do not think straight. You probably didn't either.

The "after-prom" is another name for "unsupervised party." Here's how to handle that nonsense.

Sweety, your "after-prom" will be when you get your ass home 30 minutes or less after the end of the prom, and you will probably not stay until the end anyway. You'll walk through that front door and give me a giant hug for spending three hundred dollars on that hideous sweatshop dress you'll never wear again. You can then tell me how much fun you had, and then we'll both go to sleep and get massages tomorrow morning.

If you have any inclination that your child is going to do something stupid after your denial of their wishes, you could keep his or her ass home, or insist on having the unnecessary after-prom party at *your* home, and resolve to stay up all night and supervise each and every misguided adolescent sneaky bastard until the sun comes up. They'll counter with something like, "Oh, mom, it will be soooo late by the time we leave, and you don't want me driving then, do you?" You'll then respond, "No problem, baby, I'll come and pick you up!"

You'd better be sure your little angel is not breaking the law by drinking or smoking *anything*, another supposed rite of passage on prom night. The last time I checked, you have to be 21 years old to consume alcohol in all 50 states. If you're 21 and still in high school, you've got even bigger challenges to worry about.

In many coastal areas, there's a new tradition popping up. Not only will you get to go to an after-prom to illegally consume alcoholic beverages, but you'll get to spend the entire night unsupervised on a beach, in a car, at a cheap motel, or at a stranger's house.

But, wait, there's more! You may want to buy her a bikini, because she will then toss that pricey dress in the trunk, right on top of the dirty tools, so she can visit the beach the next morning and relax. Of course, the tradition is to spend the entire next day free from any and all responsibility, because, you know, prom is such hard work. As your teenaged daughter is laying under the warm sun, know that she is in the optimum position as the millions of sperm that her unprotected date launched into her most private of places during her unsupervised after-prom rite-of-passage continually attempt to reach the ampulla of the uterine tube to fertilize one of the eggs in her ovaries. If she happens to be ovulating, prom night may have ended her educational experience altogether.

If there's any single time you are entitled to be an asshole as a parent, it's prom time. Your kid is probably ignoring you at this stage, anyway, and he or she is a year or two from leaving home. Save yourself a lifetime of grief. Contrary to whatever your kid tells you, one can live happily ever after without going to prom. I didn't go to mine, and here I am writing sarcastic prose about being a parent. If you know you're too much of a wuss to say no, call the school and find out the prom date early in the year. They should have a range of dates. Then, book a cruise for your entire family well in advance and put in for vacation at work. "Oh, honey, that's too bad, we'll be out of country on your prom day. You should have let me know earlier."

How about this – we replace proms with a star-studded gala event that praises the best science, math, history, or English students? Or, maybe a festival featuring art or cultural talents? Or a fundraising gala showcasing the creative talents of the school band and sculpturing or photography students? Or, how about any event that even remotely resembles and celebrates *education*?

Fat chance. Our society will undoubtedly continue to celebrate jocks and trendy bitches.

14: four years of beer pong

Millions of high schoolers trade in their school sweaters for rental caps and gowns as they've finished a complete presidential term. Hopefully, some of them actually learned something between the fashion shows and drama.

I was at a graduation party for my step-nephew, if there is such a thing. His uncle swung by in his brand new ghettoed-up Dodge Charger. Now in his mid-40s and remaining single and childless, many men in their redneck circle look up to him as a mentor. From the fifteen or so minutes I spent with him, in between his bragging about his stupid car and spitting tobacco, I surmised he wasn't too bright. So when he sat down to give his nephew some advice, I wasn't expecting more than a good hearty laugh. Although it was not eloquent by any means, that redneck gave his nephew some of the soundest advice I've ever heard.

He began talking about how everything you do can affect your life. How your entire life is made up of opportunities and missed opportunities. I'll paraphrase as best as I can from memory.

That artwork on your arms? That could cost you a job. That big hole in your ear that you think looks all cute? There goes a promotion. Those track marks on your arm or that THC that shows up in your blood test might make the difference between you living in a nice home or in a box under a bridge.

Now, you're gonna party and drink beer and throw up a bunch. You're gonna act stupid and senseless and pretty much be an idiot for the next four years. And all that's a given. But what you can't forget is you're in college for one single reason — to get that diploma. And it doesn't matter if you have a 2.0 or a 5.0 [sic], so long as you get that diploma is all that matters. Enjoy yourself. Everyone else will too. Just don't forget what you're there for.

The most important thing you can do is surround yourself with a whole lot of friends. Get into the books only as much as you need to, but make sure you do get out there and party. Be involved in everything you can. Be nice to everyone, even the geeks. Because you never know who might end up as a big boss somewhere, and they're more likely to hire an old friend rather than some stranger with good grades and a better resume.

That man made me wish I was thirty years younger. Shoot, I'd be running Apple by now. Our nephew had no idea how valuable this advice will be in his life. I can only hope that kid isn't half as hard-headed as I was.

As we helped move one of our children into her college dorm, I watched scores of clueless parents (of course, wearing their own college t-shirts in a desperately failing effort to remain relevant) carry plastic tubs containing their entitled child's belongings into their rooms. Disturbingly, many of their children were hanging with friends or fiendishly texting while their goofy nerd parents did all the work. Ironically, it's a safe bet that most of those bumbling parents are probably footing the complete bill for tuition, food, books, dorms, and beer runs. Lucky kids.

I talked with one of the mothers. I joked about how these kids are basically going to party for four years, on her tab. She found it offensive that I thought much of the lauded the "college experience" was a waste of time and money. After all, that particular woman got to live at college, and she still believes those were the best years of her life. She got to see Michael Jordan and his team get beat by her college basketball team, which was sadly the highlight of her life. And now, she's all the better for it. She hasn't worked a day in more than 18 years. I asked her why she felt she needed to go to college, if all she was going to do was be a stay-at-home mother. She said something about that not being her original plan, then got upset with me and excused herself. I struck a nerve, I suppose.

Thanks to one of the most successful public relations campaigns in human history, college is now big business. Our current collegiate system is a hilarious waste of time, money, and resources. Colleges are now spending millions of your tuition and tax dollars on niceties like upscale dormitories, huge football stadiums, and, believe it or not, *water parks*. One look at any college kid's Facebook or Instagram account (they've probably blocked you, so set up a new account pretending to be a fellow student) will show you endless selfies, taken while at parties, engaged in under-age drinking, general misbehavior, and in various embarrassing situations you probably don't want to know about. Our daughter was caught in a handstand doing shots against her dorm room wall. That was quite magical. These kids are having the time of their lives.

Congratulations, mom and dad, you too have fallen for the biggest scam of humanity.

Hey, I'm not alone in these seemingly crazy thoughts. Investment gurus at Goldman Sachs agree many students are better off not going to *mediocre* colleges – the ones that rank in the bottom 25% of all universities. They earn less, on average, than high school graduates. But even those who attend mid-tier universities might want to reconsider. "The average return on going to college is falling," Goldman researchers wrote. The bank is known for ruthlessly focusing on the bottom line. In 2010, the typical college student had to work 8 years to break even on their bachelor's degree investment, Goldman found. Most graduates would be around 30 years old by then.

As the price tag of a college education goes up, it's taking longer for the investment to pay off. Here's what Goldman projects:

-- 2015 graduates won't break even until age 31
-- 2030 graduates won't break even until age 33
-- 2050 graduates won't break even until age 37

Attending schools like MIT is still a huge resume and pay boost for life, but Goldman and I both wonder whether millions of students at lower-tier schools would be better off doing other kinds of training, or simply entering the workforce right after high school.

And when you consider room and board, the outlook begins to look even seedier. A friend's daughter recently came home from her *mediocre* college for the weekend. I'm still wondering why this particular girl felt it necessary to live on-campus, even though her home is only a 30-minute drive from her school. Anyway, while at dinner one night, college-girl's younger sister asked her what was the best part of college. College-girl replied "I don't have to ask anyone if I'm allowed to go to McDonalds at 9:30 at night – I can just go. Plus, I can go to parties too. I can't do that at home." The silence was deafening as I watched her father quietly conceal the $100 in fun money he was going to slip to his daughter and tuck it back into his wallet. I'm guessing he went home and cried that night, as he began to figure out where, in his recently downsized home, his hopelessly lost daughter was going to sleep once she dropped out, or worse, graduated and couldn't find a job.

However, in today's misled and maligned society, a college degree is crucially important. But the truth is, for most entry-level jobs, many of Corporate America's human resource gatekeepers don't really care *what* your degree is in or *where* it's from – only that you kowtowed to common expectations and went into indentured servitude to get that piece of paper. Human resource managers, the single most two-faced conformist group of individuals in the pool of humanity, are brainwashed to firmly believe that a college degree is the rite of passage that indicates that you aren't a budding entrepreneur, a rabble-rouser, or an innovator; and you are now ready to conform to a drone-like workforce. After all, how else are you going to pay all those student loans back? They figure they'll have you on the hook for at least a decade, well past the time it will take for your hard work to become profitable to them.

There are obvious exceptions, including cliquish little groups who wear certain colored socks, which may give preference to job candidates who have similar sheepskins. The school you choose can sometimes help give you an edge. But with the fragmentation of colleges and online options, that's becoming more of a rarity.

I agree with Goldman. But it's bigger than that. For a large contingent of college students, college may be a ridiculous waste of time and money. Your children will literally waste several *years* of their lives in typical four-year colleges, learning and doing things that have absolutely nothing to do with their major and even less to do with almost any career. I still cannot fathom what required classes in literature, history, aesthetics, or Italian will ever have to do with a job as a plumber, a nurse, a software engineer, an x-ray technician, an insurance adjuster, or an advertising buyer. No one in any administration will ever honestly explain why your kids have to take all those useless classes, other than to rack up credit hours, which you'll be forced to pay for.

Post-graduate studies are an entirely different thing. That's where you'll learn how to truly practice business, science, engineering, law, or medicine. Do yourself a favor – cheap out on college, and save towards grad school.

Now, about the most important matter. I don't remember reading anywhere in any law book that it is the *parent's* responsibility to fund four or more years of hazing, frat parties, kegs, bongs, sexual escapades, or any of the other non-educational nonsense that happens during the typical workforce preparation experience. Parents who support this notion are complete idiots, regardless of whether it was done for them or not. I'll be damned if I'm going to sacrifice my health, well-being, and retirement, as well as my child's welfare and future, to pay for four years of bullshit. You're on your own, kid. Why? First, as you've hopefully gathered by now, spoiling children does not work. Lack of responsibility does not make any child a better person. A life of leisure leads to the dangerous expectation of entitlement and laziness. Secondly, if a child invests his own money in his or her own life, they'll tend to make wiser decisions, and take life more seriously. Thirdly, if your kid can't afford to go to a "party school," he or she is more apt to actually *learn something*, even if that something is calculus or Italian. A commuter college, even a community college, seems to be a smarter choice.

I know a family who proudly sent their only son to the University of Florida during those Tim Tebow years. They paid a fortune for out-of-state tuition and accommodation, all so that their son could chase his dreams of studying sports medicine, whatever the hell that is. This kid was in heaven. And what an amazing experience he had.

UF's Gainesville campus is a tidy little place with roughly 50,000 people. It's kind of like its own little town, surrounded by beat-down strip malls and typical failed decadent suburban sprawl. Students forge life-long relationships and generally seem happy while they're there. This kid was never homesick. I can attest UF campus life certainly seemed fun, and in some ways, resembles a slice of social paradise. Hell, I wanted to live there too.

Six years later (why rush it?), graduation finally rolled around. Meathead received his lauded sports medicine degree. But rather than pursue graduate studies that might have actually led to a career in sports medicine, he decided to begin his *pseudo* fringe professional sports medicine career while hanging out in Gainesville for a little while longer. When sports medicine jobs didn't pan out, perhaps as a result of the other several thousand equally unemployed candidates who graduated before him with that exact same degree, and who also decided to remain in Partytown, USA, he finally took a job as a telemarketer.

More than a decade after Bubba first set foot in Gainesville, he was still in Gainesville, and still a telemarketer. He tells people he's in banking, since he cold-calls investors. Kudos to the capitalist schmuck who had the foresight to see Gainesville as a wonderful location for a cheap telemarketing outfit staffed with unqualified sports medicine graduates. This kid became so entrenched with his wonderful movie-like college experience, he just couldn't leave it. Mom and dad still shake their heads as they wonder why they spent nearly $100,000 in room, board, tuition, and spending money to raise a Gainesville-based telemarketer who is very well-versed in sports medicine.

I just heard that a certain Gainesville, Florida university cancels classes on football game days, as do several other institutions of higher learning. I'm still trying to figure out what football has to do with education. If that doesn't expose the college fraud, I don't know what else does.

Despite my poison tongue, not going to college in this economic environment is like getting a very pretty facial tattoo that says "Don't hire me, because I'm a loser." You have to go to college. It's a strange and sucky no-win situation.

And you should do the best you can to get into a top-tier college. College is the only single name-brand thing that matters to some folks in this world — a sheepskin from a lauded university will open many barricaded doors. That fact is entirely discriminatory, but it is what it is.

Bottom line: you've just gotta go. But be smart about it. If you've still decided you're paying for it, unless your child is a stellar genius or a scholarship-worthy athlete, opt for a local community college or a cheaper four-year experience where they can live at home. Despite Goldman's depressing advice, a low-cost local degree is better than no degree at all.

15: like a boss

Discipline is critically important in raising a child. They need to be taught that there are rules and limits in life, and there are real and sometimes dire consequences for breaking those rules. If your children don't learn this fact early, you're going to have one devil of a time trying to teach it later. And if you're foolish enough not to teach it at home, the culture shock of learning it in the real world may result in your son or daughter living on your couch, broken, depressed, and disillusioned, by the time they reach 25.

Ironically, despite what they say and their actions, children long for structure. That may be one reason gangs have such an easy time attracting inner-city children from broken homes. Gangs offer structure, and any kind structure resembles safety and security in a small mind.

Here's an important test. Do you envision yourself as one of those parents who is friends with your child? Do you consider yourself "cool" and "hip" and "one of the kids?" Do you engage in conversations on their level, and keep up with the latest trends in celebrities, music and fashion? You obviously need more to do. You're setting yourself up to become a complete failure as a parent. Put your kids up for adoption immediately before you cause any further damage.

Perhaps you are the polar opposite. Some parents would be better prison wardens than parents. Before you force your average kid to play the cello, compete in chess tournaments, or become the next fencing master, remember that kids are just kids. Without letting them run buck-wild, let them spread their wings a bit and give them an opportunity to express their own interests rather than forcing them to pursue yours. Will you run the risk of permanently alienating your children? Probably not.

You need to find a balance somewhere between the friend and the warden. It's a difficult task, since each of us is different. You'll need to consider your child's common sense, aptitude, size, shape, physical ability, age, subset of friends, and level of maturity.

Your primary job as a parent is to teach your child the difference right from wrong. Today, our children are inundated with mass media, social media, and marketing messages that have greyed and often obscured the lines between these concepts. Your task, to communicate the difference, is now more difficult than it has ever been before, in the entire history of human evolution. You need to be clever and underhand for your lessons to be effective. Observe your child's behavior, and then make predictions about future behavior in certain situations, as best you can, based on the evidence you gather. This will hopefully allow you to plant relevant and timely reverse-psychology seeds in your child's mind, which will help them make better decisions and consider real world implications and repercussions more objectively.

One not-too-bright mother made all the rookie mistakes. Beverly allowed her daughter to begin dating, unsupervised, at 14. She rarely intervened in her child's social activities, writing them off as "that's what teens do." Beverly gave her daughter a brand new car at age 16. Beverly considered herself a "cool" mom, so she decided against issuing a curfew. Beverly allowed her daughter to stay in a house that she rented the Jersey Shore, for two weeks each summer, completely unsupervised, knowing that there were older boys bringing alcoholic beverages to her daughter's parties. Any teen would think this was fabulous. Today, poor Beverly is now the gossip of all her former friends, as the loser mother who unwittingly created a substance-abusing, irresponsible, unemployable dependent on the state who has ultimately ruined her ex-husband and her daughter's life, too.

Never forget that until your child is a legal emancipated adult living away from your home, *you* are the boss. You *need* to be the boss. Regardless of what he or she says, your child subconsciously *wants* you to be the boss. Although it's easier and may seem cooler to be your child's friend, this is the single biggest mistake any parent can make. When they're grown and have families of their own, then you can be friends. But for now, your child really needs you to be in charge. Although they'll never understand or admit it, most children feel more secure when you position yourself as a figure of authority. Like a gang leader! Authority teaches them to be more responsible. This will help them become better adults and hopefully responsible parents.

Personally, I believe in a progression of freedom. When a child demonstrates to me that she can handle certain gradually more complex situations and responsibilities, and I will allow her graduated incremental freedoms. If she can't get good grades, keep her room clean, and do the dishes properly and consistently without me nagging her, she's obviously not ready to get her learners permit and certainly not prepared to party with her unsupervised friends until 1 AM. Communicate this method to your child, and make sure he or she understands exactly what is expected from them. Pay very close attention, test and evaluate frequently, and then punish or reward accordingly.

You will run into significant resistance. Many of your child's peers' parents will not enforce any rules, and your child may think your system is abnormal. Naturally, they'll become jealous. I blatantly tell my kids the truth – other parents must not care about their kids. I ask them, "Wouldn't you rather have parents who care about you?" They disagree at first to save face. But when think about this for a while, they usually agree.

Unfortunately, in America, forget about any sort of physical punishment. The paddles and leather belts many of us not-so-affectionately remember from our own childhoods have been hung up permanently. Thanks to several misguided parenting experts and overly liberal judges who have set ridiculously enabling precedents, we can't even say hurtful words that might elude to the usage of any form of physical discipline, because this too could technically be construed as assault. As a matter of fact, if a child even feels slightly threatened, no matter what kind of havoc that child has directly caused, they've been conditioned to call the police on their parents and report domestic violence. And many do. As strange as this sounds, you should be aware of this. It's quite embarrassing when the local police pull up to your home with lights and sirens to intervene in a silly family squabble.

Make sure that your children are well aware that if they call the police and you are arrested, they won't get to stay home alone. Standard operating procedure dictates the child will be immediately removed from their comfortable and familiar environment, lose most of the toys and privileges that you pay for, and they'll be placed in a potentially less attractive foster care situation. Depending on the location, they may have to change schools too. That should make them think twice about calling 911 the next time you punish them for forgetting to wash the dishes.

In some cases, sometimes through no direct fault of the parents, a child may be too far gone to recover. Instead of attempting to handle a potentially violent situation yourself, call 911 and have trained authorities intervene on your behalf. I am aware of many unfortunate situations in which this has happened. This action by his parent sent a definitive message to her child. A few other strange but real twists later, things worked out for the mom and her husband. The kid's out of the house, not breaking down any more doors, and the parents are finally rested and seem quite happy. Little Punkin' is now in rehab.

When you see parents ask their kids to do or not to do something and the child looks back and sneers, it's because our society has removed the teeth of discipline. We are now faced with at least two complete generations of humans with no fear of civil or religious retribution. Wonder why our prisons are so over-crowded? Our largely amended and now very loosely interpreted Constitution has unintentionally produced a culture of citizens who are ill-suited for civilized society.

Be that as it may, you should strive to avoid these mistakes. Know that even though your disciplinarian hands are tightly tied, there are still quite a few very effective tools in your arsenal.

Always try reasoning first. Tell them why you don't want them to do what they think they should be doing, or vice-versa. Project the long-term effects of a potentially bad decision. You may have to paraphrase several times before you get their attention. For example, your 16-year-old daughter wants to go to a nighttime beach party or bonfire with a bunch of classmates. You ask who's organizing the party, and she infers that it *may* be a student, but she *thinks* one of the parents *might* be there. Then she quickly corrects herself, and says a parent will definitely be there. You ask for the parent's phone number to verify, but of course, she doesn't happen to have it. And she insists it would be weird if you called. You decline permission on the grounds that it is technically illegal to have a party on the beach without a permit, which can only be issued to an adult. Further, it's a bad idea to be in the dark with a bunch of strangers. You know from experience that someone is likely to bring alcoholic beverages or worse, which is quite illegal. Further, mind-altering substances tend to lead to generally bad behavior which may include fights, inadvertent vandalism, and the potential arrest of all involved.

She still can't comprehend the problem, because *nothing bad ever happens* during those beach parties on any of the teen sitcoms. So you'll have to be creative and paint a relevant situation that delves further into the possibilities.

Well, sweet-ums, dark areas could be an invitation for rape. A beach is a public place, and people, like scary homeless people, may be there. Inadvertent physical harm from being in the wrong place at the wrong time during a fight, like being hit by a thrown garbage can or a broken beer bottle, could lead to *permanent* disfiguration of your face or body, and who wants a scar on their face? And an arrest on your record could hurt job opportunities or your chances to get into the college. Inexperienced teenaged minds are not yet wired to consider all these real-world circumstances, so it's your job to do the thinking for her.

Listen carefully to her response, if she offers one. Your child may have the maturity to make the right decisions, apply the right care and reasoning, and ultimately offset your concerns. Or her argument might be immature and completely invalid. Still, with this method, you need to offer your counter reasoning as a *discussion*, not as though you are laying down the law. Remember, it is your job to teach them from your experience so that they won't make potentially silly or damaging mistakes. Remind them of this fact. You might not have enough information to make an informed decision, but you do have the prerogative to decline permission based on that fact, and leave the burden of proof to your child. The delay in permission may give you enough time to avoid the potentially adverse situation.

If reasoning fails, you have the option to offer a substitute, such as a distraction. Play a game. Go to the movies. Have your own supervised beach party. Whatever. But just be a parent. Don't simply give in because you don't think you have a choice – you most certainly do. She may be mad as hell and storm up to her bedroom to fiercely defend her status on the social network of the month, but she'll get over it. Bring her some ice cream a bit later, and at least attempt to talk with her. Remind her that your decision was made for her own good, and that you love her with all your heart.

In the event that he or she has already done something stupid or disrespectful, you must show some authority immediately, or you've just green-lighted such behavior and your child will run amuck from this point forward. Yelling and showing your displeasure is typical and can be moderately effective, but that's sometimes not enough. You need to invoke immediate consequences. Depending on the severity of the infraction, you should have a predetermined and reasonable punishment ready to deploy.

Most importantly, you need to remember that they are just children, and it's completely normal for them to make mistakes – as it is completely normal for you to correct them. What is not normal or acceptable is repeated mistakes. A three-strike rule is a fair and effective method of discipline, depending on the offense. The first time, you should offer calm reasoning and steps for improvement or redemption. Strike two means you didn't make your point clearly the first time, or your children don't think you're serious. The punishment should be more severe for a second offense. A third strike, with the same bad behavior, means your child has no respect for your authority. Now it's time to get serious.

You have the power and authority to take away the things they love. You legally cannot and should never deprive them from basic needs like safety, food, shelter, and clothing – but you sure can make that supply of basic needs seem miserable. It's your hard-earned money, and you're the boss. These are just a few proven punishments that have enough teeth to show you mean business:

- *Ground them from all outside activities – except school.*
- *Increase chores – frequency and complexity.*
- *Withhold allowances.*
- *Cancel the cable TV.*
- *Cancel the data plan on their smart phone.*
- *If they need a phone, replace the smartphone with a prepaid flip phone for old people – with no smarts.*
- *Change the password to the wireless internet.*
- *Physically remove the cable modem.*
- *Sell the video game system.*
- *Hide the car keys.*
- *Remove the car battery.*
- *Let the air out of at least two car tires.*
- *Sell her car.*
- *Disallow permission to go to the prom.*
- *Don't pay for any fringe activities.*
- *Cancel vacation.*

- *Drop them off at your parents before you go on vacation.*
- *Sell the poodle.*
- *Remove their trendy clothes and shoes from their room and replace them with clean and conservative thrift store clothes.*
- *Provide bland meals, and avoid eating out.*

Punishments, although they should clearly suck, should not be unreasonable in severity or duration. Grounding a child for missing curfew should only last a week for a first offense, but let them know the next time the punishment may go on longer.

Punishments you probably should *not* dole out include:

- *Shooting their laptop on YouTube.*
- *Forcing them to stand on a street corner with a sandwich sign describing their mistake.*
- *Anything that has anything to do with duct tape.*

Discipline is a love-hate thing. Children must be taught that there are consequences for not doing the right thing. In the real world, you've got to compete against everyone else. If you go to work and decide not to do your job, someone else will do it, and the slacker will be fired. If you get fired, you won't get paid, and no one will hire you because you'll have a bad reference. If you don't have a job, it'll be difficult to pay rent, eat, buy beer, and make car payments. You'll lose your cell phone, your internet, and you won't be able to party with your employed friends. It's hard to realize this fact in the comfort of your childhood home.

Once your unemployment runs out, welfare averages about $300 a month for a single person. To put that into perspective, the average rent for a one-bedroom apartment is about $550 a month. You're already $250 in the hole, and you haven't eaten or bought toilet paper yet. Never mind your car, insurance, gas, the internet, or your cell phone. They'll all be gone – you can no longer afford those luxuries. What's that, junior? You want to move back home if things don't work out? I don't think so. There are situations that may warrant a move home, but it's always smart to make that option as undesirable as possible.

Sorry, punkin, we've already moved and downsized. Or, we converted your room into an office. Maybe you could sleep on a couch for a few nights. But we'll need to charge you rent. And you'll need to do an inordinate amount of chores to pay for your meals.

Only discipline with teeth will be effective. Make sure those kids can feel the bite. Perhaps that infant circumcision was payment in advance for all the grief some sons will inevitably cause their parents.

It's a parent's job to nag their kids. Call it what you want, but every time you attempt to steer your kids straight, you're nagging them. It doesn't matter if you've mentioned something once, twice, or a hundred times – you're still a nag. The problem is, all humans have an inner mute button. Repeated exposure to any stimulus causes desensitization. And repeated nags will go unheeded. You're wasting your breath.

What you need to do is *filter* your advice. Determine what's truly important in terms of respect and safety. For instance, a lot of things got on my mother's nerves. One of her biggies was when we didn't completely close our mouths entirely when we ate, resulting in a strange smacking noise when chewing. She routinely told us to close our mouths, yet we routinely forgot. Besides, it's hard to eat with your mouth closed, Mom. What's the big deal?

A very difficult thing for anyone to learn is how curb their advice. Ask yourself if modification of the behavior in question is really important enough to risk activating a child's inner mute button. Is the offending behavior simply something that's a pet peeve, or is it something that may directly affect their health or well-being? A better question would be, wouldn't you rather they hear you when you tell them to be careful crossing the street?

There are better ways to get your point across. One of the most effective I've used is to pull my kids into a quiet place when I see something I want to address, making sure I have their complete attention, and then I calmly explain why they should or shouldn't do a certain thing. I try to make the explanation as relevant as I possibly can, considering the child's age and level of maturity. Explaining the potential social, physical, or other pitfalls or repercussions of a certain behavior seems to be more effective in curbing future actions than a quick verbal nag. In certain circumstances, a swift and immediate, yet adequate punishment may be necessary to permanently get your point embedded into their memory banks.

Remember, children can become desensitized to any tactics, so mix them up, use them sparingly, and only use them when necessary.

16: driving me crazy

I live in a golf cart community. Basically, that means the police look the other way when you drive your $5,000 jacked-up golf cart on the public sidewalks when you're too lazy to walk or ride a bike. Supposedly, an obscure local ordinance states that you have to be 14 years of age to drive a golf cart on the sidewalk. I think that's an obvious oversight. You should have a driver's license to operate any motorized vehicle. Even with the 14-year-old rule in place, it's not uncommon to see some unsupervised 11-year-old idiot zipping around the neighborhood, showing off for his less fortunate friends. Someone's going to get hurt or killed, and that's when the law will formalize. That seems to be the American way – wait for someone to die, get voters angry, and then look like a political hero when you finally pass legislation that should have been passed when it might have saved someone.

In my old neighborhood, the stupidity of local drivers was much more lethal. It seemed to be a common rite of passage for a boy to get a pick-up truck as soon as he got his driver's license. Florida Rednecks aren't the best judge of character, and many are severely lacking in common sense. If you get a child a pick-up truck, he or she will eventually let some idiot ride in the open area in the back. A rogue pothole, speed bump, brake check, burn out, or an innocent freak accident can lead to that idiot's death. One guess whose parent will get sued, and whose kid will be charged with vehicular manslaughter.

The legal age to get a driver's license in my state is 16. Some very smart people I know made the rookie parenting mistake of giving their kids cars as soon as they got a license. Full-time access to any automobile is the ultimate freedom. The average 16 year-old is nowhere near ready for that kind of freedom. Plus, have you checked into the insurance rates for a 16-year-old male child? Better sit down with some aspirin before making that inquiry.

A car is many things. Primarily, it is an expensive yet convenient mode of transportation. But please don't pretend to be so naïve. It is also a potential *weapon*. It is an *escape* from authority and proper guidance. It is an avenue for adolescent *irresponsibility*. It is an unsupervised private place for *sexual experimentation*. Come on, you were 16 once. You must remember what it was like. If you get your child a car at 16, you can kiss that dream of your child saving his or her virginity until marriage goodbye.

In a 2005 article in USA Today, reporter Robert Davis cited the findings of brain researchers at the National Institutes of Health which show that the weak link in a teens brain is what's called "the executive branch," the part that weighs risks, makes judgments, and controls impulsive behavior. Scientists at the NIH have found that this vital area is still developing throughout our teenage years and isn't fully mature until about age 25. Evidence is mounting that a 16 year-old's brain is generally far less developed than those of teens just a few years older. Girls, and especially boys, are still quite immature and continually experimenting with sensual arousal and risk, often not yet fully aware that life is fragile and finite.

The main issue with children driving is that there are more distractions and greater peer pressure than ever before. A child's brain is worried about all kinds of temporary non-essential silliness, including image and social standing, and less concerned with the more serious consequences of life and death, especially the death of others who don't directly affect their lives. Perhaps television and movies have desensitized today's children to the injury and death of strangers, but that's a topic for an entirely different book.

There are laws in some jurisdictions that specify that there should be no cell phone usage and no passengers until a certain age or level of experience is achieved, which is a good start. But one drive to your local shopping district will easily prove these rules are frequently broken. As soon as they think you're not looking, even the most responsible teenagers with friends in a vehicle will be joking, laughing, singing, rapping, scheming, drinking, and doing other things they shouldn't be doing. What they will *not* be doing is devoting their entire attention span to the hunk of metal surrounding them that, in a single instant, could change or end their young lives. You were probably guilty of a similar digression, although you probably did not have a smartphone, a GPS, an in-dash entertainment system, or a navigation system to pull your eyes off the road.

There is a growing movement towards *graduated* drivers licenses, or GDLs. One of the limitations that applies with a GDL is a ban on night driving. Finally, legislators have come to terms with the combined factors of immaturity and darkness causing a disproportionate amount of unfortunate incidents. However, a violation of the state law is considered a misdemeanor in most states, and the lack of teeth in these laws results in them being ignored by many teens and their parents. Nighttime driving is insanely dangerous for inexperienced and immature drivers. For their own protection, and for your own sanity, man up and offer to drop them off and pick them up until they're at least 18. If their stupid friends give them a hard time, they're hanging out with the wrong people. Tell them to find better friends.

Defensive driving courses are critically important to teach a new driver how to avoid potentially deadly situations. As an added bonus, a certificate may qualify you for a discount on your insurance. Here are the best things I learned from my drivers' education class, taught by a man named Mr. Fidelity way back in the stone age.

Just because the Speed Limit is 45 does not mean you need to travel exactly at that speed. Note the word *"limit."* Contrary to popular belief, you can legally drive 37, 40, or 43 MPH in that 45 MPH zone and still keep pace with the law abiders. It is extremely dangerous to stare at your speedometer rather than the road ahead of you. Let the speeding idiots pass you. They'll clear the way of any unfortunate animals or obstacles that might be down the road. Try not to laugh as you pass them by while the policeman is writing them a ticket.

There is a real area known as your "blind spot" along the side of every vehicle, when in which you cannot see another vehicle from your side or rear-view mirrors, or a spot in which someone else cannot see you. Always double check your blind spot before switching lanes or passing someone, especially if they're in a truck. Turn your head quickly and look out your side windows.

Never assume people are always going to stop in time, move out of your way, or generally do the right thing. Everyone screws up and makes mistakes at one point or another. Especially 90-year-old men, and texting teens.

Most importantly, if you're stuck on a railroad crossing and a train is approaching, get the hell out of the car and run away. The train is not going to stop, regardless of your calculations or how much you pray. Believe me, God wants you to get out of the car too.

Limiting driving is one of the most important things you, as a parent, can and should do for any teenage boy or girl. In most cases, there are alternatives to driving that allow your child to get to school and work. Remember walking? How about bicycles? School buses serve most suburban districts. And most urban areas have public transportation, too. I didn't get my own vehicle until I was almost 19, and it didn't kill me. Riding my bicycle about 5 miles each way to school was great exercise, and I fondly remember it as an enjoyable way to start my day.

Remember, driving is a *privilege*. Since you're probably paying for the car, gas, maintenance, and insurance – and you are ultimately financially liable for any teenage stupidity – you're the boss. Don't hesitate to take those keys away if chores aren't done, in any case of disrespect towards you, or if something simply doesn't feel right. You may be saving your child's life.

17: outsourced and automated

Have to admit I am a fan of movies dealing with time travel, the future, and societal dystopia. Why? I'm looking for warning signs to protect my flock. No one can think of everything, but a little imagination combined with a collective intelligence can help formulate very effective hypotheses. My vision of the future for our children is quite dark and dysfunctional, as every prediction of a future generation has been since predicting the future has been a thing. With each successive implementation of technology, societies in general require less hard work and physical labor to survive and prosper. And for the first time ever, humans may no longer be required to think and innovate. We already have trained machines to do that for us. The hair on the back of Stephen Hawking and Elon Musk's necks is standing at attention at this premise.

Here's the thing. Technology is amazing. It has saved countless lives and allowed most of the developed world to achieve an almost ideal standard of living. Cheap and plentiful food. Widely available medical treatments. Comfortable and clean shelters and pastimes our ancestors could not have imagined. The people who invent technological advances are brilliant, as are the shrinking groups of people who have benefited financially from those advances. And therein lies the problem. Calm down, my fellow Republicans. I am not advocating redistribution or a socialist movement. However, the fundamental flaw of technology is that eventually it displaces the roles of people.

I traveled to the future in a time machine, right after Brian Williams and I came back from saving the world from North Korea and ISIS. No, smart ass, it wasn't a Delorean. Or a hot tub. I still can't believe John Cusack refused to do the second movie. Even Chevy Chase reprised his role, and he's a much bigger star. The BMW electric car I traveled in was much more suitable for time travel. It already had a fusion chamber and a flight kit.

On the civilian end, things are bleak for lower-level jobs including the only job sectors with current growth, manufacturing and service industries. Self-driving cars are expected to roll out in or about 2018. Over a million people a year are killed in automobile accidents in the United States, with even more life-altering non-fatal injuries sustained annually. A large percentage of those accidents are human error. There is no doubt the roads would be safer, assuming anti-hacking technologies are improved substantially by then. I would guess that there are nearly four million, maybe more, Americans employed as bus, truck, delivery, taxi, Uber, and limousine drivers. When self-driving technologies mature in less than a decade, in our wonderful nation where shareholder equity is more important than social responsibility, what positions do you think your favorite large companies are going to cut first? We are already seeing semi-automated trash trucks in our neighborhood. And a neighbor recently told me a tale about being romanced by automated bartenders on a cruise ship that poured and mixed perfect drinks. Apple, America's darling (and richest) company is fighting to remove child labor from its outsourced manufacturing processes with even younger workers – that run on electricity. Hospitals are not immune – medicines are already distributed by automated delivery systems, and tests are read by doctors seven different time zones away. Chances are you've called a company recently and spoke with a computer rather than a person, perhaps to the completion of your task or the resolution of your problem.

And let's look at he ultimate fall-back for underprivileged Americans – a successful twenty-year career in any branch of the United States Military. Recruiting centers tend to pop up in failing malls and shopping centers of socioeconomically disadvantaged areas, which became disadvantaged through the last rounds of societal change, labor outsourcing, or automation technologies. Now that Google and other companies are jockeying for position by purchasing or investing in companies that develop and manufacture robots and artificial intelligence (AI), what do you think will be the first application of this new technology? That's right kids, drones and robots will replace pilots and soldiers sooner than you think. It's already rolling out. You don't have to pay robots, you don't have to feed them, you won't have to provide expensive medical and retirement plans for them, and no pine box, folded flag, or survivor benefits are necessary when a robot gets killed in action. CNN reported the cost of keeping one soldier in Afghanistan for a single year was close to one million dollars. Soon, our government will be able to purchase ten robots for that figure, and use them indefinitely, or disposably.

Running further with the AI thing, we cannot be far away from computers that are capable of building more efficient machines and writing better code faster than any human could. With 3D printing already a reality, in the grand scheme of the history of civilized society, we are merely hours away from the complete automation of everything.

So, the question of the day remains: What the fuck are all of us going to do?

And there's the problem, fellow capitalists. If there are no jobs, what do you do with all the people? They all have to eat, they all require shelter, they all require medical care. But with no jobs, there's no income. And if there's no income, there can't be any income taxes, so who's going to pay the government? No worries — the whole country will simply go on unemployment. But with no tax revenues, how do you pay for those benefits? Tax the wealthy, right? Not. Politicians assume if you tax the wealthy, they'll leave for another country with greener pastures. Many prominent American investors and companies have already set up shop in tax havens like Ireland, Switzerland, or Grand Cayman.

Are you beginning to see the conundrum?

I'm not smart enough to figure this one out. What I do envision is an entirely new transformation of what we consider civilization may be required. Call it hybrid socialism, communism, whatever... I can't fathom another alternative. Business-sympathetic advisers and reporters tell us not to worry, because another industry always evolves, saving the economy, and produces millions of new careers we can't even imagine. I apologize, but I can't see how that theory will apply this time, since we're replacing people with automation. There will be very few things humans can do that robots won't do better. Even the darkest cornerstones of human civilization, slavery and prostitution, may be simulated and automated by some future capitalist genius. By 2050, there ain't gonna be jack for any of us to do, and there ain't jack any of us can do about it.

In all seriousness, I have no idea how to advise my children in their future careers. All the genius plans I had now seem irrelevant and futile. At the time of this writing, my youngest was 14, and his generation may eke by in the traditional sense of things. I told him he should build robots. But his kids will definitely be completely screwed.

Your child will hopefully succumb to the pressure to attend some sort of post-secondary education, and that is probably a good choice. One of you, either your child or yourself, may incur several thousands of dollars' worth of student loan debt. But before you let your kid run around willy-nilly and choose to be a chef, actor, jewelry designer, or an art literature major because it seems like *fun*, you might want to have a little chat about the *real* world.

When you think about it, we're churning out more and more college graduates. The world's population is increasing. Yet the job market is *constricting*. It doesn't make economic sense to hire people just for the sake of hiring people because that makes shareholders angry. So what are all these college grads going to do with their pricey sheepskins, especially in the more easily automated or outsourced industries?

Politicians and economists seem to agree that the market will "work itself out." They somehow are convinced that since the wonderful miracle of Capitalism has always created new jobs, it will continue to create new jobs, in new industries that we can't yet imagine. It is true that no one foresaw the advent of the internet and how it would change the way we get our news, consume entertainment, or shop for things we used to have to shop for in person. But those changes have created huge economies of scale for many companies and are dramatically changing the entire job market. Businesses are becoming more efficient at a larger scale. That's great news for stockholders and online shoppers, but incredibly bad news for retail workers, current job seekers, and especially for your children.

All the *experts* in career counseling (basically, superficial liars who don't really have any marketable skills or any clue what the future holds) are attempting to save their own feeble butts by steering people towards one of two obvious fields: healthcare or software. "You'll never go hungry in healthcare," says my annoying medical salesman neighbor.

Thanks to an aging population and increased cancer rates leading to record-shattering hospital bills and pharmaceutical profits, the healthcare business is indeed booming. The industry has no interest in actually *curing* people, primarily because *treating* them and extending their miserable lives with drugs and therapy is creating new millionaires daily. Many of today's lauded health practitioners aren't much more than today's pharma-whores. The New York Times once reported that pharmaceutical companies are well aware that ex-college cheerleaders make great pharmaceutical sales-folk.

As a result of the transition from brick and mortar retail to electronic shopping, as well as more tasks becoming automated, hence replacing even more unskilled workers, software engineers are in currently in high demand. Someone has to write the code that will eventually kill those jobs. Eventually, software will learn to write its own code that is better and more flawless than any manually entered text, but we're still at least a decade away from that.

You should want to steer your kid towards a worthwhile education that will lead to a worthwhile career. Aspiring towards retail management, iron chef-ing, or any sort of clerical job is career suicide in today's environment. Also, librarians, secretaries, garbage men, reporters, insurance appraisers, mailmen, and even farmers are all predicted to be extinct by 2020, due to consolidation, automation, or obsolescence. The last thing you want is your depressed and unemployed kid sleeping on your couch after college, with a worthless degree, plus a couple hundred thousand dollars in debt hanging over *your* head.

No problem, you're thinking, because your little man happens to be the hotshot running back on his peewee football team. Shoot, you think, he'll most likely be rolling in dough by the time he turns 20. Sports are wonderful pastimes, but less than 0.01 percent of high school or college kids will end up making it to paid jobs in the NFL or NBA. At least baseball has minor leagues, but fast food workers make more than those ballplayers do. No one gives a damn about ice hockey – unless you're Canadian, eh. The thick-headed redneck bubba dad enrolling his kid into football camp every summer is gambling at best. His phonetically challenged kid would have been better off at Sylvan than on grass with head trauma. The ghetto mom sending her boy to the playground in the hood with a basketball instead of tutoring him in math or science isn't really doing him any favors in most cases.

Granted, it does happen – some kids make it to the big leagues and do very well. But the much more likely failure can create an extremely discomforting situation. Insurance and automobile sales, two favorite careers of ex-college athletes, are going to be mostly online soon. You can thank to an Australian gecko, some annoying woman named Flo, and those hard-working less-athletic kids who became software engineers.

You would think this newfangled society we've created with a lack of opportunity might ensure there will be a large supply of less than fortunate volunteer soldiers for years to come. Ironically, airstrikes and drone warfare are beginning to make our armed forces a little too efficient, resulting in cutbacks at the personnel level. Soon, even the armed forces won't be an option for less fortunate kids.

Things are changing faster than they've ever changed. The job market is uncertain. Education is overpriced and commonplace, and competition is ridiculously fierce. So what's a kid to do to be successful in today's world? Well, that depends on how you and your child define *success*. Success is definitely subjective.

Success in a capitalist society is usually synonymous with being wealthy. A little hard work is usually required, but may not be necessary if you have wealthy parents. More importantly, it boils down to opportunity: access to people, things, and resources. No matter how clever or innovative you are, no man is an island. You will need to be part of a larger village, filled with a necessary supply of idiots, to prosper. If you weren't born with connections, you'll need to find them yourself. A key element is how many people you can get to *like* you at critical junctures in your life. And it sure helps if the people who like you already have contacts and resources that they're willing to share.

Superficially, what society considers *financial* success requires several traits that could be considered sociopathic. If you think about it, many of our European ancestors were adventurers who left their native lands willingly. Some completely discarded their families or obligations, back in a time when leaving home was a much more permanent endeavor. Financial success may require you to sacrifice your morals, and your time. You can always change your morals, but you'll never get back your time. People who opt to work rather than spend time with their children while they're small tend to regret that choice. As a parent, you probably won't want to make that mistake.

Wise people have learned that *personal* success is much more important than financial success. You can be hideously wealthy, yet incredibly miserable. Personal success is the balance between earning enough money to live how you would like to live, and actually enjoying your life. Some of the happiest people I know work hard at less glamorous jobs for a relatively modest wage, but they seem to enjoy what they do, and sure smile a lot at home.

Contrary to popular belief, you can teach empathy. Most wannabe well-to-do folks consider empathy to be one of the financial deadly sins, right up there next to Socialism. Empathy is nothing more than choosing to look at a situation from multiple points of view, which helps to strengthen logic and reasoning.

My son used to joke about an upcoming zombie apocalypse. I told him I thought it's already here. He asked me what I meant. I asked him what a zombie was. He described one. I asked him what the difference was between a zombie and some of his least favorite friends. The only difference he could ascertain was that zombies ate brains, and his friends didn't, as far as he knew. He began to see the light. There are those who are enlightened, and those who are not. The more of those zombies he can avoid, the better he'll do in life.

Help your child figure out what he or she considers to be successful. But don't handicap your kid by adjusting his or her future based on a low bar or any far-flung assumption – make sure he or she is well armed to deal with whatever the world throws at her. Hopefully, parents won't be automated or outsourced too.

18: i suck

Some kids, for many varied reasons – most of which are unimportant, unfounded, and often seemingly irrelevant – are scared to death of being *ridiculed*. An overwhelming sense of impending failure and self-doubt clouds their opportunities to shine and advance. How can you identify those kids? Simple. They're the ones who look exhausted from laughing the loudest when even the slightest misfortune falls upon someone else. This type of deflection can be incredibly draining.

Don't worry – insecurity is perfectly normal, and especially during childhood. I used to have my own case study at home. Comparatively, she was always one of the prettiest girls in her school – one of the few who didn't suffer through the sudden and often traumatizing physical change some girls' go through during adolescence. Regardless, this girl still thought she was ugly, or at least repeated that phrase about a thousand times, probably yearning for constant reassurance that she wasn't. What was truly remarkable about this insecure sibling was her attitude towards people. If you were nice to her, reinforcing her worth in any way, or even participating in her life as nothing more than a sympathetic ear, she had zero respect for you. None.

Conversely, her older sister was a completely disrespectful monster towards her. And yet the younger sibling seemed to accept and entirely respect that. The insecure girl worshipped her tormentor. Although I carefully broached that topic on several occasions, hoping to see a light bulb flash in her mind that I anticipated would cure her insecurity, she was continually reluctant to ever take anyone's side against her sister, in any argument. I don't know if that response was out of fear of repercussion. Even today, admittedly knowing her reaction to her sister's treatment was irrational, she still is not forthcoming when asked.

As a parent, it's your job to recognize insecurity and at least attempt to alleviate it. But what you cannot do is lose your child's respect. Like the sibling previously mentioned, insecure children seem to gravitate towards an authority figure. A berating authority figure, like the elder sibling, is definitely not healthy and can nourish the insecurity. You need to be firm but supportive, a very difficult balance to achieve.

The most important fact you can convey to a potentially insecure child is that you approve of them. Kids, especially early on, are always striving to get your approval. If they do something above and beyond the ordinary, like score an A on a test, or perform someone else's chore without asking, or actually flush the toilet, always make sure you reinforce that act both vocally and physically, with a hug or a high-five. Responsibility is a learning process, and this reinforcement will help to hard-code this positive behavior into their tiny little brains.

If they fail at something, let them know it's not the end of the world, and that you will always be there to help them succeed the next time. Sit with them and answer questions about their homework, if you can understand it yourself. Work on a project with them, but do not do it for them. Provide guidance to help them find information and resources. Find a qualified tutor when necessary. Assure them you are there to help whenever they need it.

Continually remind them that they're not alone. Everyone fails at something at one point or another. And most, if not all, of their peers are just as (or even more) insecure than they are. This is completely normal. An adolescent is in a perpetual state of change and unsure about how tall they'll be, how smart they'll be, if they'll be pretty when they grow up, will their teeth be straight, and other factors beyond anyone's control. Let them know you were there once too, and everything turned out just fine.

If they're afraid of being seen as a failure in your eyes, which is more common than you think, you may not be aware of the trouble until it's too late. Some kids get lost and just give up. When a child gives up trying to fit in, they'll exhibit signs. At first, it'll be introversion. They'll lock themselves in a room and surf the internet, or watch countless hours of senseless television. They'll isolate themselves from friends and family. You should recognize this abnormal behavior.

Then phase two kicks in. This is when your kid bums money for unsightly piercings, tattoos, and unnatural hair colors and cuts. At this point, they have given up on conforming. And once you've given up on conforming, you typically don't care about anything. Insecurity may be an early sign of depression. Nip it in the bud.

What makes a personality? Psychologists, biologists, and philosophers cannot agree, as they're all not quite sure. However, we do have several clues.

I worked with a set of identical twins for about two years. These two young ladies were born minutes apart and raised, under adverse circumstances in exactly the same environment. Their mother abandoned them at an early age, and knowing that fact can be devastating to any child.

On the surface, these twin girls could not have appeared to be more similar. But that's where the similarity ended. They were both great kids. Both were quite loquacious and very open about anything. And both had a temper, and weren't afraid to engage anyone in fisticuffs. Twin 1 was much more confident and a risk-taker. Twin 2 was a bit more introverted and studious. After initially not being able to tell the difference between the two, I began to recognize subtle differences in their voices, speech, content, motions, and character. Nature had provided the exact same genetic materials in both of these people, yet they seemed so different in many ways.

However, located somewhere in the deep recesses of their psyche, there were fundamental similarities in terms of morality. They both would never cheat on their boyfriends, and they'd never steal from anyone. But, both would agree that cheating on an assignment or a test wasn't such a horrible thing. And both would give their lives to protect their twin.

A subsequent intern I had the pleasure of working with was not a twin, but was also a model citizen. Raised in a more stable environment by two physicians, this kid may have been the black sheep of the family. How dare he pursue a career in computer engineering rather than medicine! But that didn't appear to matter to his parents, as they provided their full support to his well thought out decision. I used to think he was faking his personality, but as I got to know him, I found he was the real deal. School was his priority in life. He chose to put his social life completely on hold in an effort to achieve the best grades he could get. Who does that? And his work ethic was fastidious. Although he had a slight problem with punctuality, when he was there, he was all there and eager to assist with anything. To be a physician, like his parents, you need one heck of a work ethic.

A few years back, my ex-business partner blindly hired some young kid as a technician. He seemed nice and fairly knowledgeable. As I got to know him, I learned that he had frivolously sued his last employer and bought the trailer he lived in with the proceeds. His mother was always looking for ways to "beat the system," while her son was apparently looking for ways to beat us. What was interesting was that several of his friends from the same trailer park who also began to work for us seemed to have the same mindset. Their work ethic sucked, and they robbed us blind.

And those god-damned New Yorkers. If there's any case for nurture over nature, it's those New Yorkers. Whether there's something in the air, water, or the ground itself in the lower southeastern corner of that cursed state, its toxic effects are felt across generations and borders. I have never known a group of more selfish, pompous, rude, and narrow-minded people. There were two potatoes left on the table at Thanksgiving dinner. Three people weren't fortunate enough to get one of these delicious special potatoes, because rather than split at least one of them, the New York man took both of them and shoved them in his mouth before anyone could utter a word in protest. I confronted him about his selfish behavior, and he, with his mouth still full of potato, went on to deliver a tirade about his childhood experiences, of how he was denied a potato, and how that would never happen to him again. Apparently, New York Caveman, as he was later known, was himself an insecure, spoiled child.

What is more powerful, genetic makeup or environment? It's definitely a puzzle. I have to believe that both share an influence in creating a human personality. Fundamental emotions and values may be passed down genetically, because emotions are influenced chemically – and this could possibly be controlled by your genetic makeup. But superficial personality traits and behaviors are definitely influenced by environmental factors – especially socioeconomics. Media, friends, and examples set by parents are important influences, too. Begin your evaluation of your kid's peers by checking out their parents. And begin evaluating your own children by checking out yourself.

If you're still concerned about your child, get him or her into the school music program. Refer to the "Middle School" chapter, if you skipped it, for the reasons why music and band can help an otherwise insecure child.

19: dealing with bullies

Josh was a small kid, in high school. He guesses he weighed about 70 pounds soaking wet as a freshman. Of course, there were kids who had developed faster, but there were also a number of kids in Josh's size 5 shoes. Teens will be teens, and bullying is apparently par for the course.

Fortunately, Josh was smart. He took several advanced classes – with much bigger sophomores, juniors, and seniors, who seemed to take a liking to mini-Josh for some reason. There were a couple of kids in high school who plucked his nerves. Bullies will beat you down daily and won't cease unless you either stand up to them or stop going to school, both options which were not convenient. But everyone has their limit, even 70 pounders.

One day, Josh found an old iron rod in someone's trash which was short enough to hide in his backpack. He was determined to use it to beat the living dogsnot out of the ringleader – in self-defense, of course. Sitcoms had taught him that if he decapitated the head of the snake, the bullying would end. Josh says he actually believed that. Josh devised a plan. He watched the bully's patterns, knew where his locker was, found when he was most vulnerable, and was ready to execute the attack. Josh admits he was scared, shaking, and probably would have chickened out. Josh figured he would talk to the bully alone and give him a chance to chill, which Josh now realizes probably would have failed miserably. Fortunately, just before Josh was going to attack, one of his bigger buddies happened to walk by and playfully pounced this kid into his locker, knocking him over. The big kid rubbed Josh's small head as he walked by laughing. Josh laughed and walked away.

Suddenly, Josh was vindicated. The bully's teasing no longer bothered him. Josh's attitude changed as he began to stand up to him, slowly shutting him down. Eventually, the bully found another victim.

Josh's entire outlook changed, that day. He became uber-confident. He no longer allowed himself to become a target, and was never bullied in school again. But it doesn't always work out that way. That kid could have died, Josh might have ended up in juvie, and who knows where that could have led. Josh admits he was one of the lucky ones.

Bailey O'Neil was an 11 year-old 6th grader, in a suburban Philadelphia school, who was punched in the nose in a schoolyard, in a bullying incident, during recess. Administrators sent him back to class with an icepack. Days later, he began to suffer from seizures and was admitted to the hospital. He was placed in a medically induced coma, to allow the swelling in his brain to subside. A day before his 12th birthday, little Bailey O'Neil passed away. Before he died, Bailey told his father that he tried to walk away, but another bully pushed him into the kid who'd hit him. The bullies were reportedly suspended for two days.

And then there's Amanda Todd, a pretty 15-year-old Canadian teen who endured one torment after another, in the years leading up to her death: sexual exploitation online, cyberbullying, and a physical assault at school. Amanda made a sophomoric error at age 12 and flashed her chest to some asshole on a webcam. That asshole posted her photo all over the internet. Kids are harsh, and they never let Amanda forget it, with a constant barrage of teasing and taunting. Amanda couldn't take it any longer, and she took her own life.

Bullying happens. And it can happen in many different ways, some subtle, some very open. You, as a busy parent, may never be aware that it's happening. One of your jobs is to protect your children. You need to pay attention and be in tune with your child's moods and activities. If you suspect bullying, no matter what they tell you, he or she needs your support. You will need to recognize certain bullying warning signs, including but not limited to the following:

- *Marked change in typical behavior or personality. Appears clingy, sad, moody, angry, anxious or depressed and that mood lasts with no known cause.*
- *More insecure than usual. Talks about feeling helpless, remarks about "killing myself."*
- *Sudden aversion to friends or social media. Doesn't want to go to school.*
- *Unexplained marks, cuts, bruises and scrapes. Afraid to ride the school bus.*
- *Unexplained headaches or stomach aches.*
- *Difficulty sleeping.*
- *Loss of clothes, school supplies, electronics, clothing, lunches, or money*
- *Sudden and significant drop in grades. Difficulty focusing and concentrating.*
- *Bullies siblings or younger kids.*

You will probably have to ask leading questions to get your child to feel confident or safe enough to open up. Ask them about tears in clothing, missing items, mood swings, or bruises. If you're paying attention, you'll know if something is not quite right. If your child won't talk to you, check with a teacher or someone else at school, who might have a clue. Subtly ask your kid's friends what's going on. Tell your kid that you are always there to talk, and it's your job to help. If you can't get anywhere, but you suspect something is wrong, seek the help of a trained mental health professional, sooner rather than later.

A friend mentioned that his son being bullied in the local middle school. I can personally attest that children in middle school, and especially the male varietal, are the worst jerks they'll ever be. My friend is no wuss — he's actually a big, scary looking dude. And his kid isn't all that small either. His son got wrapped up with the wrong bunch of idiots, and his life is miserable. His son is depressed and hates going to school. His grades are suffering. Fortunately, he has spoken with his father about it. At least he has a vent. When Josh told his own father he was bullied in middle school, he laughed at him and smacked him around a bit to teach him a lesson.

Unfortunately, no matter what you do, no matter what your school administrators say, and no matter what threats are implemented by school districts, city governments, and state law enforcement, you are often powerless to fight bullying. You have no authority as a parent, and the bullies know this. You can't beat it, because you can't go to school with your children to protect them. The world is not yet mature enough to tolerate smart, small, weak, or quiet humans.

I can summarize my advice to him in one single word: MOVE. You have no choice if you want to save your child. Get him or her out of the situation the moment you become aware of it. Move out of town if you can. Change school districts. Home or virtual school your child for a few years. It sounds dramatic, but this may save your child's confidence — or his or her life.

Lamar Hawkins' mother arrived at the school to pick up her son about 5 p.m. Wednesday, but he wasn't there. At about 7 p.m., the family went to law enforcement to report the boy missing. Deputies searched the family's neighborhood and surrounding area. When they began searching the school, they found the boy. Lamar, who was small for his age, committed suicide at Greenwood Lakes Middle School in Lake Mary, Florida after being bullied, Morgan said. The boy's mother, Shaniqua Hawkins, fought back tears at a news conference and blamed bullies for pushing her son over the edge, saying she tried doing everything possible to help him. Her husband, Lamar Hawkins Sr., sat by her side. The mother said she felt paralyzed by the inability to stop the bullying. "It was a feeling I hope no other parent has to fear," she said. "They won, because he took his life as a result." Had they moved their boy, he might still be here.

Tricia Norman, whose 12-year-old daughter, Rebecca Sedwick, jumped to her death in September 2013 from a tower at an abandoned cement plant in Lakeland, Florida after months of alleged cyberbullying might have been able to save her daughter had she known about the bullying and pulled the plug.

Now, if you suspect *your* little angel *is* the bully, you need to collar that prick as soon as possible. Bullying laws are finally beginning to pop up with zero tolerance policies, holding you as a parent legally or financially accountable. Having a child who's thrown out of school can be socially embarrassing and financially inconvenient for you, the parent. Hopefully, you've taught your kids to do the right thing, and this will never be an issue.

Olivia Black

20: baggage

"My life used to be better, before you got here," said the insecure teen girl to her well-intentioned stepfather. Out of nowhere, she produced that well-aimed dagger and plunged it directly through his heart. This was more than six years after her mother and this man had begun their relationship. Although the stepfather hadn't formally adopted his wife's daughter, he had fully accepted her as though she were his daughter, treating and spoiling her not unlike he would his own biological children. "We used to be closer, us and mommy," she continued. Apparently, this teenaged girl had forgotten the fact that she had been a mere seven years old the last time her mom was single, and seven year-olds typically do require and receive much more attention from moms than teens. Apparently, her memories were frozen in time, and the spoils of the past six years didn't matter.

"You weren't like this before. You changed," said the confused 11-year-old boy to his father in the same household. "Before you married her, you didn't make me do chores." Just maybe it was because he was 4 back then, and couldn't yet reach the washing machine.

Something I call *sibling shock* introduces this kind of silliness you'll face in today's blended family. With the divorce rate hovering at or above 50%, chances are good you might be involved in a step-parenting or dual step-parenting situation at some point in your parental career. Although you had no biological responsibility for your partner's offspring, you have entered into an unwritten agreement to be physically, mentally, and financially responsible for the upbringing of your partner's child as well as any of your own. And, as an added bonus, you'll be forced to interact with ex-spouses as your step-kids, giddy with glee and with bags packed, are immediately released from whatever menial chores you assigned whenever bio-Daddy or Mommy, the part-time parent and child's absentee hero, walks through your front door.

In most cases, there'll be a primary parenting situation, where one parent will be largely responsible for just about everything. The other parent gets to ride in on a silver horse every other weekend and steal your children away for fun and frolic, only to return them after a day or so when shit starts to get real. Mothers are typically the primary parent, but there are more and more fathers stepping up.

Being a step-parent is always a complicated situation, especially when blending children from each side. The only reasons the Brady Bunch worked so perfectly are because the other parents were dead, and each completely fictional scenario was always neatly tied up at the end of twenty-five minutes.

If I had to sum up being a step-parent in one word, I'd have to choose "awkward." There are so many moments when you're not sure what to do, fearing stepping on paternal or maternal toes. You will always have to choose your words very carefully, and make sure you never join in the estranged parent's dissing sessions, because you do not and never will have the standing to do so. The downside is that you, as a step, will typically never garner the respect the biological parent would receive. Unless you formally adopt, you'll always be viewed as "mom's boyfriend" or "dad's girlfriend," and your standing will be similar to that of an aunt, uncle, or adult family friend. Prepare yourself for the inevitable "I don't have to listen to you, you're not my dad" as the biological parent you're replacing smugly chuckles in the background. Prepare to become a full-time caretaker with zero emotional reward. You'll have to be strong and disciplined enough to deal with this kind of stress. Hopefully, your partner is worth the trouble.

It is important to set your baseline for respect immediately. It is a delicate balance that has much to do with the age of the children at the time you've stepped in, and the age of the children when the biological parents separated. If you're a very serious retired drill sergeant and you hook up with a woman who has two teenagers who just separated two months ago, chances are you'll be scorned eternally. Conversely, if you come in as the fun and laid back friendly sort, the kids probably won't respect you. You have to find a balance to achieve respect: the sweet spot at which you will be tolerated and you will have at least some authority over the children. It is critically important that the biological parent fully and vocally supports whatever you both decide your authority will be. Talk it out away from your children – never have this conversation in front of them. The most important thing is to communicate with each other honestly. If her kid is being an asshole towards you behind Mom's back, don't let it fester. Tell Mom and demand that she immediately steps in, and discipline when necessary. The only way you'll have a chance to succeed as a family unit is if all parents show unity – let them know early and often that dad and mom are unwaveringly on the same page.

Jake walked into a situation with two young girls, aged 8 and 9. Mom had been divorced for about a year, and their dad was still part of their lives. He was a commercial pilot, so his presence was scarce, leaving Jake to fill in the majority of the daddy duties. At this age, Jake felt it was important to have a certain level of respect and authority if, for nothing else, the girls' safety. "Don't stand on that chair." "Don't drown your sister." "Don't beat your dog with that iron rod." But the girls would always look at their mom whenever Jake said anything, and mom never backed him up. Eventually, Jake became pissed, and that led to a rift between he and Mom. Her blind eye and lack of support allowed her kids turn into monsters over the next year, as Jake's typically gentle counseling eventually turned into yelling. And Jake is definitely not a yeller. After they divorced, Jake called her ex and had a beer with him to discuss what a maniacal twisted woman their collective ex-wife was.

There are quite a few situations where, no matter what you do, the step and child simply won't ever mesh. This tends to be more prevalent when the child is an older teen. For example, a 14-year-old girl might be mad that Mom left Dad, and she would resent Jesus Christ if he walked into Mom's life. You have to remember that children have relatively few real or relevant life experiences to draw from. For years, movies, books and television shows have brainwashed kids into thinking life is a perfect little story. When something goes wrong, a step-parent gets to play the part of the evil person who has ended that fantasy.

Some kids can be very troublesome, requiring an inordinate amount of time and energy that you may not have to give. Other children are simply perpetual asses. What you have to do is decide whether your relationship with their biological parent is strong enough to overcome the sometimes hefty baggage that comes with it.

There are success stories. Jake's following step situation was filled with mutual love, joy, and respect. He gained two lovely step-daughters, whom he gladly accepted as if they were his own; and although he's quite difficult at times, she adores his son with all her heart. They do have hang-ups and difficulties and sibling rivalries (both biological and step) at times, just like any other family, but overall, they have a strong family unit everyone seems to cherish.

If you're the only one with baggage, it's *your* job to make the situation successful.

A boy I know lives with his mother and grandmother. They're nice folks, but Grandmom lost Grandpa recently, so she's still adjusting. The equilibrium of their household shifted dramatically when Grandpa passed away. Today, Grandma is doing her own thing and not paying much attention to her grandson. The boy would mouth off to her, which is rude and unacceptable behavior. Grandma let him get away with it. His mother is a traveling sales person, so she's away from home frequently. And when she is home, she's not always really there. Her Bluetooth earpiece is now permanently attached to her brain.

When his mother is home, she feels guilty for being away so much. Since she has no other man in her life, she spoils her son with all kinds of electronic trinkets. When they walk through Target, he points at something, and it almost always ends up in her cart. Mom is unknowingly creating a monster. This kid is running around doing whatever he wants to do with little to no supervision. And that's just not healthy for a little man. When he goes to his father's house and attempts to settle into Dad's safe little nuclear step-family environment, his son is usually belligerent for several days before he settles down.

At Dad's home, both Dad and Stepmother pay lots of attention to him. He doesn't have many friends in Dad's neighborhood, so he stays inside the home for the most part. They enjoy family dinners, games, movies, and… *chores.* Since Dad's more organized activities interfere with the freedom he's used to having, obviously they have some challenges.

This type of situation occurs frequently in today's blended families. You can't control what happens at the other home. But you can set things straight at *your* home.

It's rare that a baggage situation goes down without any problems. What's important is that you stick to your guns and make sure your children know that your home has its own rules, and he or she damn well better comply when they're there. Stepchildren will undoubtedly complain and make sometimes hurtful statements about preferring the much looser household, but that's too bad.

Remember – step-children are an important part of the package deal. Thankfully, children are transient. They'll grow up and hopefully leave home, so you and your partner can eventually enjoy each other. But the time in between can be very trying.

And there is always the possibility that some kids will never leave home. You won't have this problem, because you've read my book.

21: sibling warfare

Peggy and Kate were about five years apart in age. Peggy, the oldest, had always treated Kate like a subhuman schmuck. Predictably, Kate idolized her older sister. The moment anyone, be that a stranger, parent, or sibling, said anything even mildly offensive to Peggy, Kate was the first person to defend her. It wasn't uncommon for Kate to treat her mother, father, and anyone else with disrespect and disdain. But Kate never once raised her voice towards Peggy. One day, I mentioned my observation to Kate, hoping she would see that she ironically esteemed the person who treated her poorly. My intent was to plant the seed that would help Kate avoid potentially caustic relationships in her future. Epic fail. I think the situation actually got worse. As is typical in any abusive relationship, when you beat someone down for long enough, they become ambivalent. It's expected. It's acceptable. And eventually, it's *wanted*. Apparently, 14 years of abuse was long enough for silly little Kate to feel she needed to defend her abuser. I figured she was pretty much screwed up for life, and recommended therapy to her mother.

One day, Kate woke up from her conscious slumber and a light bulb went off in her mind. She realized that her sister was rather bitchy, and that she was wasting her time in idolizing her. Kate's entire perspective turned around, that day, and Kate now had her shit together. Kate had newly found confidence, friends, and a direction in life. Peggy was still trying to find herself, living in the desperate shadows of her lackluster boyfriend.

A few months later, Kate fell back into her funk. There she was, once again defending her evil abusive sister. It happens more often than you think.

Sibling rivalry and disagreements are completely normal, and may be healthy in many cases. Your children will learn to master critical corporate skills including indirect insulting, excusable sarcasm, deflecting blame, avoiding responsibility, and, hopefully, compromise and negotiation. You, as the parent, will need to be the judge, jury, and/or mediator.

Contrary to what you might believe, the oldest sibling may not always be the dominant one. A younger brother or sister may be smarter, bigger, faster, better looking, or, if nothing else, they may appear to excel in certain categories a sibling considers temporally important. This will really upset the older kid, although you may never be aware of this. Elder children assume they should logically be better at everything and get to do everything first, but it doesn't always work out that way.

The middle child complex is a real malady. Your older children tend to have relatively complex needs, and we amateur parents typically spend much more time figuring how to fulfill those needs the first time around. Your younger children require a different type of more frequent and immediate attention. This often leaves middle children in a situation in which he or she may feel left out, even if they're really not, leading to insecurity and sometimes depression. Make sure you recognize this situation, which will usually, but not always, be evidenced by one or more episodes of angry and ostensibly illogical temper tantrums. Ensure your middle kids believe they're getting the attention they too deserve. This may be as simple as a few frequent reminders like, "See? I did *your* laundry too. And I fed you your favorite meal. And I didn't forget to pick you up from school today!"

Step-siblings are a growing category. Mixed families are very common, and may introduce what *sibling shock* into your child's previously cozy narcissistic environment, as discussed in the prior chapter on Baggage. Your youngest may suddenly be thrust into the middle child position, and adjustments may be difficult due to timing, jealousy, and associated childhood insecurities. Just be sure to keep this in mind and discuss it with your partner and the affected children.

22: electronic parenting

Things change quickly in this fast-paced crazy world. You'll need to keep up with technological trends to stay relevant, and to fully understand the opportunities and threats that will present themselves to you and your children.

There was a day, and it wasn't all that long ago, when my children used to play board games with me. My girls would read, draw, play guitar, and enjoy crafts such as painting, sewing, and candle making. And I have photographs and video to prove it. There were so many smiles and flourishing laughter. We talked. We bonded. We shared life. But things changed. The world changed. Our time together, whether due to these changes or their growing up or a combination of both, is drastically different. Something happened to our family. It was a subtle tragedy I would wish upon no one.

It was Christmas morning 2008. The sun had just peeked over the horizon as our children gathered around our Christmas tree in their new pajamas with warm cups of hot cocoa topped with a ridiculous amount of marshmallows and whipped cream. The boy was the last one down. He stayed up late on Christmas Eve to watch a movie with me. The kids were filled with anticipation, eagerly waiting to tear into what Santa had left them under the tree before half-eating a giant chocolate chip cookie and leaving most of his milk to curdle. Apparently, Santa is lactose intolerant. There were still fake snowflakes and a few puddles from those that had melted near the garage door, which Santa uses at our house since we live in Florida and don't have a chimney. We smiled as we gave the go-ahead nod to our wide-eyed children. Each of them went for the smallest box first, hoping, praying, and anticipating that the number one item on all three of their Christmas lists was in that small package. Unfortunately, it was. The oldest one shrieked as she saw it first.

Looking back, that moment may have been my single biggest parenting mistake ever. Little did I know I had just engineered the end of our cohesive little family. December 26th, 2008 became the first day of the era in which we now refer to as *A.D.*, or *Apple Digitali*. All days prior to that day are now known as *B.I.* — *Before Internet*. Thanks, Mr. Jobs. You ruined my board game nights. Sure, there were game consoles and portable units. But it was a tedious effort to get new games. You had to physically go to a store to purchase or rent one, and the financial investment allowed parents to postpone purchases until a birthday or holiday. And, the limited content got boring quickly. With today's handhelds, content is available immediately, and new apps come out daily. Most are free upfront, requiring inexpensive immediately downloadable in-game purchases to move forward, all while attached to Mom's unlimited credit card.

Today, most family's board games sit in the same spot they've been for nearly a decade, probably coated with a thick cover of dust, now buried under several pounds of other unused toys and discarded gifts. Jake and his son used to fish and take bicycle adventures to collect geckos to transplant to his yard to help with pest control. Jake and his son haven't gone fishing in years. You may find it is very difficult to get anyone to leave the house for a walk, bike ride, or any form of exercise. Surprisingly, our children now become annoyed at the talk of vacation, and *especially* cruise vacations because there's no unlimited internet on the seas (actually, there is, but we refuse to purchase it). Any form of digital disconnection is frowned upon and complained about to the point of being physically painful. I call this affliction *computer cramps*.

Fortunately, for my family, it was more of a gradual change than a culture shock. Since I was fortunate enough to know someone in the technology business, we were early adopters to portable technology, so many of our kids' friends hadn't yet hopped on the digital bandwagon. Due to limited content and connectivity, our portable devices began as a temporary diversion used on long car rides or to pass time on the toilet. But as the rest of the sheep followed our example, very soon thereafter, the device replaced our family time. No one talked with each other unless prodded. No one took their eyes off their device. It became a social stigma to not have a smartphone, or worse, not have the *right* smartphone.

I long for the days of B.I. Hopefully, our kids will age out of this phase and remember that we're still here — while we are still here. I am planning to foster a retro movement – where it's not cool to have a digital device. We'll see how that goes. I'm guessing that'll crash and burn, but it's worth a shot.

Digital disconnection is not the worst problems today's parent will face. A much larger and more ominous battle looms on the horizon of every American household.

I was walking through a mall with my family, and noticed a life-sized cutout of Justin Bieber. People were stopping and taking photographs next to the cutout. I did too. Looking into it a little further, I realized exactly what the cutout was advertising – Justin Bieber's new *cologne*. Apparently, people can attempt to elevate their social status by lathering up with chemicals derived from the sweat and urine of goats or pigs while pretending to smell like JB, Jay Z, J-Lo, and even MJ – that's Michael *Jordan*, not Jackson. I have to wonder if the Michael Jordan cologne was modeled on his pre- or post-game odor. The scary thing is people actually buy this stuff. A *lot* of people buy this stuff. It was on that day I became angry with pop culture, and I realized there was a fundamental problem. Conspiracy theorists, although often wacky and unfounded, have stumbled upon some valid concerns. They argue that there are some very wealthy people who want to remain very wealthy, so they're driving American civilization into stupidity. Here's what's obvious.

Television, the pseudo-parent of today's busy generation, has created a mindless group of followers – children who all feel compelled to watch the same low standard of programming in order to stay relevant with their like-minded peers. I've tried yet continually fail to find a manner to objectify or even accurately describe this phenomenon. Conspiracy-minded critics call it a frightening display off what seems to be mass-hypnosis. They may not be far off. Whatever you call it, it is difficult to deny that corporate media behemoths have created an entertainment culture in which individuality is frowned upon, and academic excellence is social suicide. When you immerse yourself into this culture, you too may uncover some fairly sophisticated and powerful psychological methods to repress education, individuality, ambition, cooperation, leadership, respect, and all the other worthwhile qualities that you'd think the model nation of the free world should emphasize.

I certainly hope freedom isn't becoming *free-dumb*, but it sure is beginning to look that way. Every generation, since the beginning of time, has surmised that the next one will fail because their lives are too easy. My parents said the same thing, as did theirs. But, speaking as the old person in the room now, this time, it *is* different. Our society has systematically engineered an entire generation of lazy and entitled humans by removing the perception of failure and all the teeth of discipline. Today, lax attitudes and ghetto-slang English are widely accepted as the norm, and they are enthusiastically defended with not so much more than the overly simple and inexplicably effective media-driven statement that stops critics in their tracks, *haters gonna hate*.

Think about it. Academics and true heroes are ignored, while people with names like Puff Daddy, Jay Z, and will.i.am are revered as geniuses. Engineered pop stars like Justin Bieber, Miley Cyrus, and Kelly Clarkson are teen heroes. Grown men who play games with bats, clubs, balls, and nets are some of the most wealthy folks in the world. And what's most disturbing is that people who have become famous for *nothing*, I'm looking at you, Kim Kardashian and Paris Hilton, have become multi-millionaires and industry titans.

Why? Because we were collectively told that's what we're *supposed* to do, and we follow like sheep. Whatever media titans tell us to listen to, we listen to. Whatever celebrities wear, we wear. When the machine determines something is *hot*, we line up and beg the machine to take our money. I challenge you to find another valid argument why thousands of people will wait in line, sometimes over several nights, to see a movie, watch a pop concert, or acquire the next portable electronic device that has a picture of an apple on the back of it.

And if you happen to fall behind in this fast-paced silliness, you are guaranteed to be chastised and ridiculed – often to your face – by strangers, your friends, co-workers, peers, and often your own extended family. Don't you dare carry a Coach purse in a Michael Kors world, or use an Android smartphone in an Apple stronghold, or certain people may refuse to be seen around you. If you can't afford it, don't make excuses. Simply get another credit card, because fashion is now super-important.

I realize I may have aggrandized a bit, but in some circles, things are truly that ridiculous. This social stigma is not only misguided and disgusting, but it's downright frightening. You can thank the bastardized work of Sigmund Freud's nephew, Edward Bernays, for validating this type of sheepish behavior.

For your children to succeed, what you must not do is allow them to become slaves to this marketing and psychological machine. Once they're brainwashed, it becomes very difficult, if not impossible, for you or anyone else to pull them away. A child's brain is developing from the moment they are born. Once they're able to visually focus, a few months into their ride, they begin to absorb stimuli from their environment. Think of the average American household: a large television, constantly showing some kind of fast-paced nonsense that is interrupted by four to six commercials every fifteen to twenty minutes. The stereo in most cars is blasting an assortment of poorly written songs, now largely spoken poorly, with some DJ spewing useless pop culture nonsense, and more obnoxious commercials telling you what you need. On the road to school and at any shopping plaza, you'll find even more advertisements. And everywhere you go, there is a barrage of electronic stimulation disguised as toys or learning aids. It isn't difficult to ascertain why so many of us are diagnosed as scatterbrained – which has been classified as an official medical affliction and is now known as ADD or ADHD.

When you think about it, through a very slow process of evolution, nature has carefully crafted the human mind to live a much simpler hunter-gatherer existence over the past forty-or-so thousand years. Yet, over the tiny window of the past *hundred* or so years, we've simply discarded all of nature's brilliant evolution and quickly changed the entire paradigm of human civilization. This has resulted in an overstimulation of our slowly evolving organic brains. In school and then adulthood, it's no wonder children find it difficult to manage all this stimulation. This leads to all sorts of mistakes in life, including critical errors in time management. Time management is one of the most important tools to success in business and in your personal life. Experts may disagree, since technology has rendered civilization more efficient, which results in more *spare* time. The twist is you now have much more to time to manage, which requires more thought.

This same paradigm has altered the behavior of parents, too. Instead of combined families living in large villages with several generations all lending a hand, as was the norm for thousands of years, we have been convinced the everyone needs to have their own individual dwelling. Obviously, this means there is duplication in furniture, appliances, utilities, borrowing, building, and necessities that led to additional expenses (and corporate profits). Additional expenses require additional income, which means both Mom and Dad have to work, spending more time away from the home, and away from traditional parenting roles.

An unsupervised latchkey child gets bored, and then on goes the television. And it's a safe bet to assume they're not watching the Discovery or History Channel – not that those channels actually run many educational or historical programs any longer. In their defense, even silliness like *Pawn Stars* and *Ice Road Truckers* provide better real-world information than today's teen-based sitcoms. The current teen show formula goes something like this:

- *Find a few child actors who can hopefully sing and dance*
- *Build a set that emulates a wealthy white person's home*
- *Insert children into a largely unsupervised surreal situation*
- *Add gobs of sarcastic and disrespectful dialogue*
- *Mix canned laughter after every other line*
- *Tie up situation neatly in 24 minutes*
- *Run two minutes of stupid commercials for useless adolescent-skewed products three times during program*
- *Cancel show when child actor reaches puberty and begins to act like an idiot in his or her personal life*
- *Replace actors, change names, adjust scripts slightly, wash, lather, rinse, repeat.*

Sit down and watch these shows yourself, and think about them from a child's perspective. What is important to realize is that these shows are molding your child's brain. Disrespectful and sarcastic dialogue has likely become your child's normal dialogue, and you'll begin to realize where certain offensive phrases originated. You, as a responsible parent, will caution them against speaking in such a manner. Of course, they won't understand why, because *everyone else talks that way.*

The surreal, often lush sets and surroundings found on these shows almost always show a large, clean, and well decorated suburban home. Regardless of where you're from this, will become what your child will consider normal living conditions. Your more modest and comfortably tidy two-bedroom urban apartment could become a source of depression.

And finally, when your kids' teenage situations don't always tie up neatly every twenty-four minutes, because there are very few social miracles in the real world, you can imagine how your children will feel.

And now, streaming services like Netflix, Hulu, Amazon Prime and others make even more programming available on-demand whenever your children wants it. If you haven't set a parental guide and password on your streaming media account, your child may be able to watch R or worse rated movies that his or her fragile little mind simply isn't ready for. You probably don't want your ten-year-old daughter watching a horror slasher film or Fifty Shades of Grey while you're at work.

I met a young man who was a junior in high school, and he asked for my help on a science project. He seemed very humble and well spoken, so I agreed. As we chatted about various things, he mentioned he had never seen many of the popular teen shows that his friends talked about at the magnet high school he attended. I asked if he thought it affected his social life, and he admitted he felt left out sometimes. But he seemed genuinely happy with his situation. He passed his time reading, studying, and working out, and he watched various documentaries and crime shows with his parents. He avoided much of pop culture, opting instead for sci-fi movies and video games. His parents work a lot and are quite well off, so it could have been easy for this young man to fall off track. Today, this young man is a well-adjusted and gainfully employed software engineer who studied on a full scholarship at a very expensive technical university.

Another high school senior needed to do an internship for one of her high school courses. She lived with her father in a very modest home. They couldn't afford cable TV or high speed internet. It was a treat for her to use the internet at school or at the office. She too read, worked out, got a job, and studied hard during her teen years.

Although this woman had some issues commonly associated with her socioeconomic status, she worked her way through college and is a senior with a promising future as of this writing.

One of the most popular boys at our local high school seemed to have it all. He was tall, fairly good looking, and well-spoken. He always wore the latest styles and blasted the hottest rap songs from his pick-up truck. But this kid was raised on Nickelodeon and the Disney Channel. He could name any character or well-known line from any popular sitcom or movie, and was familiar with every silly butt-shaking dance featured in rap videos. Unfortunately, his memory wasn't quite as keen on remembering historical events, literary rules, or mathematic definitions. He graduated with average grades, but that didn't seem to matter to him. However, when high school ended, so did his apparent stardom. He took some time off, and then eventually got a job at a fast food restaurant. He did attend a few semesters at community college, but dropped out. He is still a nice kid, but he has no direction and no goals.

Jake too grew up in front of a television. Dad worked a bunch, and Mom was an uninterested stay at home mother. But that was in the 1970s, in the days of more wholesome entertainment when writers were still persuaded to write scripts with more moral themes. Two of his favorite shows were The Brady Bunch and The Courtship of Eddie's Father, shows that demonstrated that true happiness could be achieved even in adverse situations. The Bradys lived in a pretty sweet split-level suburban pad, and they had a maid. And Eddie was a penthouse dweller, with a Japanese housekeeper. The kids were always supervised by some adult figure, often the hired help. From his earliest years, Jake had aspirations of getting out of the ghetto, because ghettoes are not the norm, according to these shows. Unfortunately, Jake still doesn't have a maid or a butler.

Is embracing today's pop culture the dividing line between success and mediocrity? I can't yet verify that with scientific certainty, and my evidence thus far certainly seems superficial. But the more people I talk to, the more it seems to be lining up that way. You decide.

23: crutches

I have to laugh when I think of certain devoted parents I know personally catering to their child's every whim. I couldn't imagine what it would be like to be my child's bitch. And parents who willingly subject themselves to that role are even more befuddling. It's got to be the fluoride.

One quiet Sunday morning, I was bicycling through an upper-class development envying the beautiful landscaped gardens that many of these homes displayed. I'm sure each of these uppity homeowners hired a landscaping firm to keep their lawns and foliage this tidy. As we turned a corner, we saw someone weeding the front flowerbed. It was a teenage boy, who couldn't have been more than fourteen. He had a bucket and a shovel, and was diligently pulling grass and weeds from wherever they didn't belong. As we passed by, he turned and smiled at us, as if he was actually enjoying his chore. I was so moved by this surreal movie-like experience, I nearly fell off my bicycle and puked. I wanted to meet these parents, learn more about their parenting style, and congratulate them on doing the right thing. Of course, there could have been a horrific backstory involving organized crime, drugs, whores, and murder that ultimately resulted in this kid working against his wishes, but I chose not to think that because I'm an optimist – half the time, anyway.

In the real world, people have to work to earn. Those earnings allow us to purchase necessities like food, clothing, shelter, utilities, gas, insurance, and other great stuff. So why would you teach your child that all those things are free? That's not an appropriate way to ready any child for the sometimes cruel and harsh real world. As a matter of fact, the shock of leaving a comfortable environment and transitioning into something that's not quite as easy may be a leading cause of depression in young adults.

The thought of touching someone else's dishes disgusted Princess, or at least that's what she had her parents think. Her family sympathized and adjusted their entire chore schedule so Princess would never have to touch someone else's dishes again. A few months later, Princess got a job at a local restaurant, working as a hostess. Ironically, one of Princess's duties happened to be clearing off dirty plates from tables and taking them to the kitchen. When Princess' parents met her boss, they were shocked to learn Princess didn't seem to have a problem touching these plates, even though they'd been used by strangers. So why did Princess find it acceptable to clean the plates of complete strangers, while she couldn't load her own family's plates into their dishwasher? *"Because I get paid for it,"* she explained.

Mull that over for a while, and you'll begin to understand my frustration.

Your child's adult work ethic will begin in your home and will primarily be taught by you. But many parents go soft on their kids as they strive for the approval of their children, or to avoid the persistent complaining and conflict that may accompany asking this entitled generation to do anything. This is a critical mistake made by many of today's parents. Forging a strong work ethic early on is another critical lesson that will lead to a better and more successful future, regardless of how you define success.

Many parents are tempted to play the hero. We anxiously await some sort of mishap or accident, then swoop in, clad in armor, riding our perfectly groomed white horse, to save the day. The only reward we ask is the smile of our helpless little victims. Don't expect a thank you, as that little being will run back to watching television or whatever useless thing he or she was doing before the mishap that you're now responsible for dealing with occurred. Give your child the opportunity to figure out a resolution to *their* problem. Coach them to learn from it, so that they will know how to handle similar problems in the real world. This will hopefully teach them to avoid making the same mistakes repeatedly. By jumping in and automatically resolving all the issues yourself, you're unknowingly providing a crutch that will never be removed. Cut the cord as soon as reasonably possible. Never miss an opportunity to coach your children and point out what can make them better.

One of our own little Rockefeller's chores was to vacuum the entire house. He was the youngest child, and vacuuming is presumably the easiest chore, requiring the least skill and responsibility. Granted, it was a fairly large two-story house, but this weekly task shouldn't take more than 20 minutes when done efficiently. As Rockefeller got a little older, we began to point out things that would make his task slightly more complicated, but lead to a better overall result. He was big enough to move the kitchen chairs completely out of the way instead of circumnavigating them to better access the crumb-laden area under the table. Rockefeller hated this, but he succumbed. We lauded his efforts as he began to do this himself. Call me crazy, but I could see an inkling of pride as he finished his weekly chore.

We have a small dog. She's basically a mutt, with one part Yorkie and the other Shelte. Her temperament is wonderful. She's very smart, fun, and energetic. But her undersized Yorkie bladder leaves much to be desired. If you don't take that bitch out once an hour on the hour, expect a new spot on your carpet. With all the other responsibilities that come with being a parent, author, and business owner, ain't nobody got time for that. I told my kids that the dog is now *their* responsibility. I warned them that if I found one more pee-pee stain on my carpet, the dog was going to the pound, where she'd probably be euthanized. That might have been a little heavy. And I made it a *family* chore – I made it clear that it didn't matter *who* took her out, as long as *someone* took her out. I was hoping to foster a sense of cooperation and responsibility. As I mistakenly stepped in a warm puddle of dog pee, I realized my little plan had failed. I made a big fuss and called a family meeting, at which I announced that the dog was heading to the kennel. I packed all her toys up and loaded them all into the car as my panicking children promptly shed all the alligator tears they could conjure. I really dropped her off at my father-in-law's house for a pre-arranged vacation, but the kids didn't know that.

The next day was oddly quiet. I couldn't tell if the kids were angry or sad. They immediately went back to immersing themselves into their electronic devices, just as they had while the dog was here. No one said a word about the dog until about a week later, when one of them stated that she missed her. And even that statement wasn't more than a passing thought. I then realized my kids didn't care! My plan had failed miserably. And now I had to go pick up the dog and bring her back home, which was going to make me look like a schmuck. But all was not lost. Now I had a new target that I could ransom which I knew would be much more effective – those damned *electronic devices*.

A good way to instill a strong work ethic is to explain how the real world works and how your child can take advantage of this. Compare and contrast two fictional candidates for a job. The first candidate does exactly what he or she is told, and not much more. A second candidate regularly goes out of her way to complete beneficial actions that are above and beyond her responsibilities – not only double and triple checking to ensure her primary job was done correctly, but doing it with a smile, showing pride in her work, and also performing tasks she wasn't specifically asked to do. Invoke a little role play here, and ask your child if he or she were boss, which candidate would they hire? Then sit back and watch the gears grind as you enjoy the positive influence you just instilled into their little malleable minds. Your results probably won't be quite as dramatic, as mine weren't, but hopefully it'll wedge in their brain somewhere.

Teach them the value of hard work. Your best bet is to assign each child a chore. The chore should be appropriate to the child's age, maturity, and physical build. If your kid isn't quite tall enough to reach the sink, he probably shouldn't be doing dishes just yet. Graduate them into new and more difficult challenges whenever they're ready.

Quality assurance is very important in the real world, so you will need to stress that any assigned chores must be done thoroughly and correctly. Otherwise the chore will need to be redone. A child might blow through doing dishes, leaving yucky food particles on plates or silverware, or neglecting to dry and put away washed pots and pans. This is unacceptable. Use the *S.E.R.R.* method to resolve these failures. **Share** the failures with them. **Explain** why they're failures. Help them **resolve** those failures. Then have them **repeat** the chore again until it is correct. I pronounce it like "sir," only with a long and drawn out and

166

sometimes annoying emphasis on the double R at the end to underscore the *repeat* thing.

There are plenty of progressively more difficult things to do that any child can safely help with if you've properly trained and supervised them. Here is a list of various things that children can do around the home.

- *Keep bedroom clean and tidy*
- *Pick up bags, cans, glasses, and personal belongings*
- *Empty bedroom and bathroom trash cans*
- *Vacuum carpets and sweep floors*
- *Mop wet areas*
- *Rinse dishes, load and unload dishwasher*
- *Wash, dry, and fold laundry*
- *Wash windows*
- *Dust tables, counters, lamps, decorations, and electronics*
- *Put trash and recycling on the curb, on appropriate days*
- *Weed flower beds*
- *Feed, water, bathe, and care for pets*
- *Clean toilets, bathtubs, sinks, and shower stalls (age 14 or older)*
- *Mow and edge lawn (best if age 16 or older)*
- *Anything else that constitutes "doing the right thing."*

The last chore on the list is the most important one. If they see a piece of trash laying on the floor, a wet towel placed somewhere it shouldn't be, or bathroom stuff left on the bottom of the stairs to be carried up, your child must be trained not to ignore it, but to *do the right thing* — and without you asking. It's purely common sense. We frequently set up situations like this and allow our children to encounter them, to test them. If we see them do the right thing, we compliment them. If they miss it, we let them know, and inform them they have not demonstrated an appropriate level of responsibility. The next time they ask for something or to do something they want to do, we remind them of the list of common sense things they failed to do, and that we base our decisions on their level of maturity as evidenced by the weight of their successes and failures.

Should you give them an allowance? It is a good way to teach kids the value of money. Instead of creating the illusion that your money supply is endless, like the Federal Reserve does, teach your children how financial transactions work. It is an important lesson, teaching them that once their money is gone, it's gone until they can earn some more. Let them know that part of their allowance includes things that may appear transparent to them – like food, hot water, air conditioning, beds, blankets, pillows, clothing, smart phone data plans, access to your home internet, and cable television. Failure to complete chores is like failing to go to work. As a result, they will not only earn no allowance, but also possibly suffer a loss of some other utility until their work has been satisfactorily completed.

You may face significant resistance. In our house, it was not uncommon to hear things like "But I didn't use those dishes, so why do I have to wash them?" Or, "I didn't make that mess, so why do I have to clean it up?" Or, "Can't I just do *my own* laundry?" Interestingly, those same chores were done with glee and zero complaints when one of our kids was at a friend's or relative's house whenever asked. And, as mentioned previously, Princess felt it would be acceptable to clean dishes at a restaurant because she got *paid* there. Apparently, feeding, clothing, and sheltering Princess isn't considered adequate payment.

One night, after witnessing behavior I considered disrespectful, I grabbed a piece of paper and wrote each of our children a bill for dinner that night. "That's about what you would pay for food and drink like this at a restaurant. And don't forget my tip." I then collected all the cell phones and told them, "I don't use these phones, so why do I have to pay for them?" Finally, I unplugged the internet and the cable television, because since I would do all the chores that night, I was the only one entitled to "get paid." The looks on their faces were priceless. They were chore free, but they were left bored without being able to enjoy their favorite pastimes.

The kids eventually recognized the error of their ways, apologized, and have not complained about doing chores (at least within my earshot) since.

Don't prop your children up any more than they need to be propped up. You don't want to train them to use crutches if they're not necessary.

24: any port in a storm

Sure, it's embarrassing. But it's how you and I got here. It's how our parents got here. It's how we all got here. It's an animal urge and a desire that may have been imparted unto us by mistake, a coincidence, your favorite god, or some other intelligent designer. You can fight it all you want, but sooner or later, your children are going to have to deal with urges, stains in their underwear, STDs, and the possibility of offspring.

You may have learned about sex from your peers in middle school. That's where most of my generation picked up its information — that certain classmate who had an older brother or sister who was on the promiscuous side, and the second or third hand whispers which followed. Back in the day, sex in movies was still censored for the most part, and there was no internet. Sex was a mystery.

Today, the internet is our world's Sodom and Gomorrah. With little more than a few quick clicks, your child's brain could be permanently wired with some deviant's form of sexual normalcy. Information on how to deal with your child's unfamiliar new feelings should be disseminated, sooner than later, by you rather than the lies and fantasies of some fictional movie or porn website. And with the next big bang of pop culture, which is probably already on Netflix as you're reading this, I am completely convinced you do not want your sons and daughters learning that 50 shades of anything is even remotely close to normal sexual behavior.

Common sense can and often does filter out garbage information. But as discussed previously, once something hits the media, we are conditioned to believe it and accept it as normal. And that is the problem. There is no filter or mechanism to ensure children realize the difference between fact and fiction.

But aren't parents supposed to have that talk about the birds and the bees with their children? Most parents find the discussion awkward, and many avoid it altogether. For those who chose to brave the topic, many teens interrupt the discussion, pretending they already knew everything there is to know because they too were embarrassed to discuss the single most natural thing humans do. As a society, we seem to be accepting this easy way out.

In Fremont, California, a health textbook that talks about masturbation, foreplay and erotic touch, among other sexual education topics, was introduced to the dismay of concerned parents who felt this was inappropriate for their ninth grade children. "There's a section that tells you how to talk to your prospective partners about your sexual history," said a parent and school district employee who may sue the district if it does not remove the book. "How does that relate to a 14-year-old kid? I don't see it at all," asked a hopelessly naïve parent. Hopefully, that child is sheltered from the internet, radio, television, magazines in supermarkets, billboards, advertisements, and the world in general.

According to a 2012 survey by hercampus.com, over 30% of college women lost their virginity by age 17. That's nearly one in three women who had sex before leaving high school. Sure, you can pretend your kid isn't fooling around, but how would you really know? Chances are he or she is not going to tell you the truth until it's too late. Shouldn't your child be aware of the life-altering and unmitigated stakes of having sex including heartbreak, the age of consent, rape, STDs, and pregnancy?

Unless you want to become the youngest grandparent on the block, and some folks actually embrace that, you should talk to your children about sex and its risks. They'll hate it at first, but persevere. Someday, they may thank you.

When are they ready for "the talk?" A better question might be, have you already missed that window? Any blanks you leave opened will be graciously filled in by your child's extremely immature, irresponsible, and misled peers. I have found that instead of giving them "the talk," some parents feel better writing it down, reading a book together, or watching an educational video. This way, you won't have to worry about missing or forgetting something in the midst of discomfort. And, they'll have an opportunity to repeatedly peruse your wisdom, whenever necessary.

Basically, the young human mating ritual goes as follows: illegally drink copious amounts of liquor to cloud all sense of reasoning. Then, against better judgment, continue with poor mating choice. Eventually arrive upon some semblance of common sense, discard poor mate, then repeat the process.

A young girl of today, thinking she's simply entitled to a boy who looks like a pop star and is going to fulfill her fairytale relationship is already in the process looking for her soul mate by the age of 12. And she may be ready, willing, and able to do whatever she has to do to get the best looking boy in school (because teen show producers have inadvertently taught her that's exactly what she is supposed to do).

Of course, boys are already ridiculously horny at about 13 or 14, as a result of Mother Nature's hormonal confusion. And media-influenced peer pressure makes things even worse.

So we're left with a paradox – silly teenage girls looking for a perfect boy and a life-long relationship. And boys who are solely interested in notching their belts to improve their bragging rights. You can tell your daughter this is how it is until you're blue in the face, and she's going to think you're stupid and out of touch.

Most average men are addicted to sex, because it feels good. Really good. And really good, *really fast*. It's very difficult for a man to have bad sex. "Any port in a storm," as the late-great Davis Brown once told me about his days in the United States Navy while deployed somewhere in Asia. I'm not really sure I want to know exactly what Davis was talking about, but I believe I got the gist.

Honestly, society needs to remove the taboo placed on masturbation for both men and women. Lots of money, grief, and unwanted children could be avoided by simply telling your boys and girls that it is completely acceptable and absolutely *normal* to take matters into their own hands. Men come so quickly they might not know the difference between hands and not hands.

Another important tip – *you* provide the condoms. Yes, even for your daughters. The stigma attached to a young person purchasing condoms at a supermarket, especially when the cashier is as young as 14 and potentially one of your child's classmates, well, you can imagine how limiting that might be. The moment you have the slightest inkling your male or female child is even thinking about sleeping with someone, *you* take care of this chore. Place them in an opaque brown paper bag and deposit them somewhere in your child's room. Write a small note, and leave it in the bag, asking your child to "Please be safe. Pulling out and the 'rhythm method' simply don't work as means to avoid pregnancy, and neither will they stop the transmittance of any STD." No further discussion is necessary.

In the real world, your daughter will be surprised to find many women don't enjoy casual sex. It often hurts, it's messy, and women are so cerebral it takes her an inordinate time to achieve orgasm – and that's only if she's lucky enough to have an experienced partner with any empathy and skills. Inexperienced young women have no idea that normal coitus won't usually lead to orgasm. It's a Hollywood fairytale, kids. Most women need a comprehensive mental workup, followed by at least an hour of foreplay, and then followed by various kinds of oral, physical, and mental stimulation that are vastly different from anything most inexperienced adolescent boys are capable of providing.

From the moment your daughter allows that nasty, self-absorbed, one-eyed monster to get into her wonderfully warm cave, she must immediately consider the fact that there's always the possibility that she might be creating her next generation, no matter how careful she might think she's being. And that subsequent generation will most likely be living in *your* home, consuming a majority of your time, money, and other resources, tacking on an additional 18 to 30 years to your parental chores. Tell your kids, male or female, that it's irresponsible to have sexual relations if you're not ready to raise a child. And it's inconsiderate and disrespectful to have relations with someone you're not fairly certain you'd like to partner with for at least 18 years to raise that child. Lots of people tend to overlook that very important fact during the heat of the moment. I sure as hell have.

And ladies, feign all the lack of responsibility you'd like, but unless you've been forcibly raped, which is horrible and unforgiveable, the decision to have intercourse is ultimately yours. Warn your daughter to keep her legs closed, no matter how much he sweet talks her, until she has at least a year or two of history with him, and she really knows him. A human brain isn't fully developed until she's about 25, and kids are not yet capable of good judgment. Your daughter won't want to hear this, but tell her don't worry about losing him over sex. If he leaves because she won't give him what he wants, he wasn't worth it. Let some other loser girl deal with his insecurities.

What's really disturbing is the current trend of teenage girls offering their *anus* as an alternative to avoid pregnancy. There is no man in this world worthy of the exit-only interface, young ladies. Unless, of course, that's your thing. It typically take quite a few boyfriends before you'll figure that out. Besides, she won't want to be labeled as "someone who takes it in the ass" by a boy who can't keep his mouth shut. At this age, most cannot. And good luck bucking that reputation.

Boys will brag about oral sex too. One blow job with the wrong guy and you'll be branded as a whore, and you'll have to live with a ruined reputation for your entire high school experience.

This is along the lines of the conversation you need to have with your teenage daughters. Here are the cold, hard facts you'll need to cover.

Honey, relationships are never like they are on TV or in any movie. If Hollywood story relationships were like the real world, they'd be depressing, and no one would want to see movies about them. Do you recall ever seeing a well-dressed welfare mom with a racially mixed child living in the projects looking for food on any adolescent-skewed cable network? No, and you never will.

Boys under the age of 30 are simply not wired to be interested in long-term relationships, regardless of what they tell you, and how well they fake it. Boys will lie, cheat, and steal to get into a girl's pants. Unlike you, boys feel ZERO remorse whatsoever for breaking a girl's heart. They'll laugh at a girl who's crying. Every single secret you tell a boy in confidence – be assured he's going to tell his buddies, and they're going to laugh at you, too. Good looking boys, especially athletes, are the worst offenders. They have many more opportunities to be with various girls, so they're less likely to value your heart or your relationship, because there's always some other dumb chick waiting.

There are quite a few nasty little bugs that can harm you, or even kill you, called sexually transmitted diseases, or STDs, that you could catch from an infected boy. You can't see these diseases, you can't taste them, and you can't smell them. You'll never know he's infected until it's too late. Even if you think you know that boy well, there is the possibility that he may not know he's infected, so never take his word for it. The only way to know for sure is to have a doctor do a test. Some of those diseases do not have a cure. That will mess up your life because you'll have to tell all your boyfriends in the future that you have a STD, and they'll avoid you forever. The only way to avoid catching an STD is to not have sex with someone unless you're sure he's clean. Condoms are effective, but they're not perfect. They can rip or slip off fairly easily.

Some girls go on the pill, which is a drug you need a doctor's prescription for that's supposed to stop women from becoming pregnant. But that won't protect you from STDs.

If you get pregnant, YOU will be stuck with the child, and the boy will continue to party. No young boy wants to be a father, especially to another man's child. There is a very high probability that he will not marry you, and even if he does, he won't stick around.

Several studies and books including "The Role of the Father in Child Development" by Michael E. Lamb, several citations indicate that young men are less likely to stick around to raise a child, largely due to socioeconomic factors. And even in our ultra-free liberal modern society, a young girl with a child is still looked upon as a whore by her neighbors, friends, relatives, and potential suitors. Society is a harsh judge of character. Continue your conversation.

A young girl with a child will be shunned by truly good boys and miss many fun social opportunities. A young girl with a child will find it incredibly difficult to finish school or begin a career, cultivating a life of mediocrity or poverty. Babies require full-time attention for at least ten years, so kiss most of your social life goodbye until you're "old," like your mom.

Alcohol and marijuana have been proven to impair your judgment. As little as one beer can devastate your common sense and defenses. It's OK to say no. If it's not OK, you're hanging with the wrong people. It only takes one poorly thought-out mistake to ruin your life.

So, my little angel, keep your legs crossed and your mouth closed until your second or third year of college. By then, if you've paid attention, you should have learned how to recognize the difference between good guys and bad guys from the stupid mistakes other students and your friends have made. I'm not saying don't date and don't fall in love. I'm saying avoid the more permanent things until you're old enough, mature enough, and responsible enough to handle the real world. Because when the world comes crashing down on you, Mickey, Cody, Cory, Carly, Charlie, Hannah, Zack, Zoey, or 'the Situation' ain't gonna be there to help.

If you really do feel the need for speed, go online and buy yourself a vibrator. My First Jack Rabbit vibrator runs about $40 at AdamAndEve.com. Plus, they ship in plain brown unmarked envelopes, so no one will know what's in it. Your Auntie Jen, Heather, Holly, and quite a few of our neighbors have them, so it's *nothing to be embarrassed about. I have one too. No, you can't try mine, because that's just gross. When you're a little older, let me know and I'll order one for you. No one has to know. You may never need a man again.*

My son is an adolescent. One of his friends is light years past him and already has a girlfriend. My son thinks his friend has become weird, since he has suddenly decided to skip Xbox beasting and Airsoft battles, opting instead to watch a movie with some girl. *Ewwwww.* Personally, I think that kid's parents are exercising extremely bad judgment for allowing their son to date at twelve. And I know for a fact his goofball father will never give his son the "birds and bees" talk.

I don't want to blow his mind, but I don't want to sugar-coat it either. This information is critically important. As with anything a parent does effectively, you need to infuse a bit of spin to make sure your well-rehearsed points are communicated succinctly and digested properly. Your talk has to be cleverly interesting and not embarrassing, two tall orders in this particular realm. I need to reverse myself from my girl talk and explain to my son why he will want to have sex so badly. I realize I'll have to be very careful in choosing my words, because they will become gospel in the event of any mistake. I needed to craft my speech with a cup of brutal honesty, a teaspoon of spin, and at least four pints of outs.

Son, eventually, if you haven't already, you will begin to have strange feelings... down there. For some reason none of us may ever know, all men are hardwired to reproduce. And that's what sex is for — the instinctual human urge to create more human beings. You already know that thing men pee-pee with is called a penis. And when your body is ready, which will probably be soon, your penis will also be capable of delivering sperm. That's basically baby seeds.

You will begin to look at women differently, and your relationships with them will seem awkward. You'll eventually want to kiss some of your girl friends on the lips hoping they might become your girlfriend. Although you are completely in control of your actions, you won't be able to control the desire that's in your head. And that is completely normal. But society and the law will expect you to control your actions. More on that in a bit.

You won't find everyone attractive, and not everyone will find you attractive. There will be a look, a smell, a sound, or some words that will engage your gears. You'll know it when it happens. Your heart will feel funny. Your face will become flush. Your brain might begin to malfunction, causing you to think about some girl all the time. Occasionally, a girl will feel the same way. Other times, she just won't be that into you, and that's normal too. Don't take it personally, and just move on. That's where "there are other fish in the sea" comes from.

Some women will find you attractive, and when you get much older, some may want to have sex with you. That's where the trouble begins. Sex is putting your penis into her vagina. A girl's vagina is a small hole located about where your penis is. I'm not going to lie to you — for a man, it feels incredibly good. It's hard to explain. But all kinds of bad things can happen when you put your penis into a vagina.

There are quite a few nasty little bugs that can harm you, or even kill you, called sexually transmitted diseases, or STDs, that you could catch from an infected woman. You can't see these diseases, you can't taste them, and you can't smell them. You'll never know she's infected until it's too late. Even if you think you know this woman well, there is the possibility that she may not know she's infected, so don't take her word for it. The only way to know for sure is to have a doctor do a test. Some of those diseases do not have a cure. That will mess up your life because you'll have to tell all your girlfriends in the future that you have a STD, and they'll avoid you forever.

Or, your sperm could attach to one of her eggs and create a baby. The last thing you want to do as a teenager is become a parent. Just because she carries the baby in no way gets you off the hook. If that child is yours, you have a moral, social, ethical, and financial responsibility to help raise that child that you cannot walk away from. Regardless if you and the baby's mother stay together, you will be responsible for paying child support until your child becomes an adult. That's 18 to 26 years in some states. And some women will avoid men who already have children. If you have a child before you're ready for that kind of responsibility, it may ruin your whole life. So just don't.

There's something called birth control. Condoms, or rubbers, are rubber bags you put on your penis to keep the sperm from leaking into a girl's vagina. They will also protect you and her from most STDs. Make sure you've got one with you before you get into a sticky situation, because once you've started to get into a sexual situation, it's very hard to stop. If you're too embarrassed to buy condoms, that's no problem, I'll do it for you. No one else has to know.

It is important to know that sometimes condoms can leak or break. Some girls go on the pill, which is a drug that's supposed to stop women from becoming pregnant. But that won't protect you from STDs. Some girls just say they're on the pill, and they're really not. It's impossible for you to know. What is important to know is that no form of birth control is perfect, and there is always the chance of contracting an STD or getting a girl pregnant. An abortion is where a doctor basically sucks or scrapes an unborn baby out of a girl's uterus, killing the fetus. They are often dangerous for the woman, very expensive, and difficult to get. So always use a condom no matter what.

Again, some of the women you find attractive won't want to have sex with you. You may be able to convince her otherwise, but you can never force someone to like you or have sex with you. That's called rape, and you can go to jail for that. For a long time. I know dudes do it in the movies, but even if you force a girl to kiss you, that may be construed as sexual assault. You can go to jail for that too. The rule of thumb is keep your hands off her unless you're positive she's okay with it. Movies are not real.

Most women's minds and bodies don't need to have sex like you think you do. Between the ages of 17 and 25, a woman will have sex more frequently for one or more of these three primary reasons: experimenting, bragging, or making babies. And ain't nobody got time for any of that… except for the first reason. That's the funnest.

Even if a woman seems to love having sex now, that won't last forever. Everything gets old. You'll probably tire of her long before she tires of you. That's normal too. Although, if you've chosen well, your woman will most likely be monogamous. That means she won't sleep around with your friends. But you're a man, and you'll undoubtedly will find you will begin to have the desire to spread your seed to other pastures. That's why God created internet porn and titty bars.

Typical adolescent males will think about sex up to fifty times a day. That will definitely cloud your mind and judgment making it difficult to concentrate on school, or anything for that matter. Also, it's dangerous to walk into a situation with a loaded gun, especially when you're going on your first dates. At times, you may find it necessary to clear the chamber. Masturbation is basically, um, taking matters into your own hands. Some guys claim to do it two or three times a day. Women do it too. No matter what your stupid friends might say, it is perfectly normal and very safe. Just don't leave towels or socks around for your mom to clean up, because that's just nasty. Just let me know when you need me to run to the store for more hand cream and tissues.

Maybe the best way to describe how quickly things can go to hell is to tell the story of Jack and Amber. I've changed the names and embellished the story a bit, although not too much. The story is so wild it didn't need much tweaking.

Jack had an inkling his hot little girlfriend was a substance abuser. They dated off and on, more off than on, for about six years. When they got back together, shortly before their daughter was born, Jack thought Amber had kicked her habit. Both Amber and Amber's mother told Jack that Amber had been in rehab. It seemed legit, so he believed them. At that time, Jack's naiveté did not allow him to realize that you never really kick a substance abuse problem. He later learned that all substance abusers are very convincing sociopathic liars.

Long story short – Amber got pregnant. The timing sort of matched up, so Jack manned-up and married her. He believed it wasn't that baby's fault that she was brought into this world, so the least he could do was give the kid a chance.

Jack's friends and family thought he was nuts. "Get a DNA test! Are you stupid?" But he refused. To Jack, DNA didn't matter. Honor was more important to him. Jack decided this was his daughter, and that he would always love her as his daughter, and that's all that mattered to him.

What still bothers Jack the most is that Amber may have abused substances during her pregnancy, which may have led to potential health issues for his child. Jack found several crack vials hidden in a closet and in Amber's bedroom during her pregnancy. Amber denied using. But she denied everything. She always has. She still does.

One night, after a tumultuous several months of arguments over Amber pawning his daughter off to her grandmother every day and night, Amber tried to stab Jack with a large chef's knife during an unprovoked, drug-induced rage. Jack managed to disarm her, with a chair.

Amber went for another knife, but Jack slammed her hand in the drawer before she could grab one. Amber then ran to the bedroom and called the police, telling them that Jack was an intruder and he was trying to kill her.

Jack thought about leaving, but that might have validated her story. So he waited outside. Lying face down with a mouth full of grass on the front lawn, handcuffed with a policeman's boot firmly on his neck, Jack noticed about ten police cars all with guns drawn and every neighbor for blocks around staring at him. Jack decided that that moment might be a good time to finally leave Amber.

Fortunately, the officer in charge took one look at Amber's extremely dilated pupils and noticed her erratically slurred speech, and then gave Jack five minutes to grab his clothes, while they restrained Amber.

A day or two later, some dude named "Jimmy" called Jack, supposedly from prison, to tell him Amber was a bigger crack whore than Jack thought. Jimmy said she was working for some big syndicate, but she turned informant. Jimmy also said one of the dealers was the baby's biological father. This was way too much for Jack to digest. Jack didn't want to believe Jimmy. Jack asked for proof, thinking Jimmy would never be able to supply it. Jack hung up and proceeded to continue healing the wounds from his already destroyed life. Jimmy called back and told Jack he'd have proof soon enough.

The next day, there was a knock at Jack's parent's front door. When he went to answer it, no one was there. But there was a poster lying on the porch, wrapped in brown paper surrounded by a thin rubber band. Jack hesitated, feeling a great deal of trepidation, knowing that this could be a pivotal moment in his life that might cause a downward spiral from which he may never recover. But Jack opened the poster anyway. And there she was – in full color – Amber, his child's mother, butt-naked and spread-eagle on someone else's bed. Jack's heart sank as this hideous reality he had been denying for years suddenly became real. Jack later found Jimmy sent the same poster to Amber's neighbors, her extended family, her church, and a copy to her school's principal. Jack burned his copy immediately.

To this day, twenty-some years later, Jack is not certain that his daughter is his biological child. Jack and his daughter are now estranged, thanks to Amber and her continued fabulously convincing fictional fabrications. Amber has told Jack several times, usually during heated arguments, that Jack's daughter is not his child. Jack will never know which words to believe from that woman's mouth. She is the only one who will ever know the truth.

Jack says he has no regrets, and chooses to be an optimist. But I bet if Jack could have that night back twenty-some years ago, he would have been at the bar with his buddies rather than with that psychotic crack ho.

Several years later, Jack remarried. Another decade later, still gun-shy but a bit smarter, he was talked into having a second child in a more traditional way. And as irony would have it, that turned into a crash and burn, too. At least Jack is fairly sure that child is biologically his.

We are human. Therefore, we are fallible. Ensure that you and your children enter every situation with widely open eyes, collecting all the information they can, and then sleeping on it. Tell them to make the best judgment they can, before they make a decision that will affect the rest of their (and your future child's) life.

25: new-trition

There are a few not-so-secret secrets to success in today's society. And no, none of them are in that silly Secret book or video. What a bunch of hooey. These are the honest and true secrets to prosperity in American culture.

The first secret reads that today, any sort of average is unacceptable. You need to be excellent in everything you decide to do. Mediocrity means failure. No-brainer, right?

Secondly, it's not what you know, it's who you... well, you get the drift. Find that right crowd, most of whom are probably the truly annoying geeky nerd kids during high school. Stick it out – if you can. One or more of them may be able to give you a leg up someday, but only if they remember you being a true friend when it mattered.

Finally, for men, it's not about the color of your skin, how good looking you are, what you're driving or the watch you're wearing — it's the amount of ozone you're inhaling that will gauge how high you'll elevate. It seems everyone needs someone to look up to — *literally*. And the taller you are, the easier your life will be. I couldn't seem to get this fact through my pint-sized son's thick head as I attempted to get him to throw down at least three glasses of hormone-induced cow's milk (or at least calcium-fortified orange juice) each day. I must admit, I found myself beaming proudly as he argued with the cunning of a seasoned attorney, albeit while at the height of an average Oompa Loompa.

Fortunately, his father is about average height. He wears 32×32 jeans, which are the shortest of all his friends who average about 6'2". Personally, I have always wondered what the mystique or attraction was with tall men. I have studied, quizzed, tested, chastised and tortured tall folk for decades. And these are my conclusions.

For some reason I will never understand, the primary qualifier in a woman's mind is the size of a man's inseam. Back in high school and college, it was commonplace to see tall men surrounded by the opposite sex. It seems people clamor to be around tall people as if it helps them elevate their own social standing.

Tall men always seem get the pick of the litter when it comes to women. Perhaps it's engrained in her fairytale mind that her prince must be capable of heroically retrieving that obscure can of corn from the uppermost shelf in order to enhance her future offspring's chances of survival. Maybe women have secret fetishes involving giraffes. Tall guys can't quite put their abnormally long fingers on it, but they ain't arguing either. What's truly interesting is that women will tend to discard all prerequisites in lieu of height. Thank goodness for sloppy seconds.

Over the years, various surveys have recorded women's preferences in certain traits found in men. Studies routinely find that a high income, a deep voice, and great shoes are important to certain women when choosing a mate. But the biological jackpot is purely physical. It seems some women love very tall men over anything else. Why? The Journal of Family Issues finds a woman thinks a taller man makes her feel safe, and/or more femine.

Here's the thing. Today's average American male is about 5'9" tall while the average female is 5'4". The average heel is roughly 3" high, meaning that even the average guy still stands two inches taller than the average woman in heels, even without his shoes. Nearly half of all women prefer a man who is taller than she. Fortunately, the other half doesn't seem to have the same preference, or would not admit that they do. Ironically, regardless of her height and the difference between her height and a prospective suitor's height, a man of average height or less may not seem to be attractive enough for many women.

Apparently, the perfect height has been cited in various studies and fictional accounts at about 6'2". This presents a fundamental problem of supply and demand. Although half of the population of adult men are as tall or taller than the average height, the remainder are shorter. And with each inch of additional height above average, the slice of the statistical pie of taller suiters becomes logarithmically smaller. Since taller men are in such high demand, the share of the population of taller men who are available for courting is disproportionately small.

There are several advantages for a woman who manages to capture the heart of a taller man. Throughout history, height has been proven to show a high correlation with success in business. There is some truth to a taller man providing some additional level of security from a deterrence standpoint. Subjectively, a taller man may also provide a social edge for an insecure or narcissistic woman.

Another curious thing I found studying tall guys is that they're entirely too laid back. Conceivably, the reason may be they've never had to fight for anything. No one picks on them because they're large. And there is always a ready supply of clueless broads eager to keep them satisfied.

The tall gene is very prominent in Anglo families. I'm not quite sure what the British are eating, but it's providing *hellagrowth* in their offspring. And since the current English-speaking world is dominated with Anglo influence, there are apparently special chairs reserved at the adult table for tall Anglos. If you did a slideshow of the top 100 CEOs in

America and Europe, you'd find their fair-skinned faces morph together almost seamlessly.

Tall people seem to do better with less effort. Sure, you can still break into that old boy's club if you're short, but you'll have to work twice as hard. What you need to do is simply become as tall as you can.

My adolescent son hated to eat. I warned him that his body is "programming" itself to prepare for a certain food intake. Part of that preparation is analyzing the availability of nutrition during adolescence, which may directly correlate to how large your body determines you should be. I warned him that he will need to eat better if he wants to achieve his goal of being six feet tall.

During early adolescence, your children will grow to about 20% of their final adult height and gain 50% of their adult weight. Growth and change is rapid during this period, so their requirements for all nutrients increase. This is especially true of calcium and iron. If your child's eating habits are less than ideal, they can be difficult to correct at this stage. Give your kids information about the consequences of a poor diet, including lackluster appearance, poor athletic ability, low energy, and less enjoyment of life. These are more important to most teens than long-term health. Make them aware that less sweets will lead to less weight gain. Calcium may help him grow taller, so he'll need to finish his milk. Protein will help build healthy muscle.

I continually remind him that he will only get one chance to help his body reach its full potential, and then it's done for life. No go-backs. No do-overs. No mulligans. Listen to me boy, and do it now, while you still can. Thanking me someday is in so many ways so much better than him getting slapped with an annual "I told you so." So shut up and drink your milk. As a matter of fact, go get another.

Little DeShawn typically ate cereal for breakfast. Then, it was chicken nuggets for lunch. Chicken nuggets for a snack. Chicken nuggets for dinner. This went on for at least the entire two years that I knew him. I once thought he was going to turn into a giant talking chicken nugget, and I was convinced I'd make millions as his agent. Somehow, DeShawn looked healthy and happy, and he managed at least a six-inch growth spurt before his twelfth birthday. All on not much more than chicken nuggets, and milk.

I am not a trained nutritionist. Not many of us know much about nutrition. Common sense would mandate that all high schools would make nutrition a mandatory class. Unfortunately, as you've already ascertained, our schools are lacking in common sense.

How did we transition from an agricultural superpower to the pre-packaged food generation over the span of just 100 years? Most of us, left to our own devices in the event of a food shortage caused as the result of a mass catastrophe like a hurricane, major earthquake, war, terrorist attack, or even a truckers strike, wouldn't have a clue what to eat or how to prepare it. The entire civilized human race has been softened and is ill-prepared for anything uncivilized. Conspiracy theorists have fathomed that large political campaign contributors demand that our children remain dependent on food provided only by big corporations. Locally grown vendors are making inroads lately, but they're still niche at best.

As with every other thankless responsibility you'll shoulder as a parent, there's always an underlying psychological element that will trash even the best made plans. The strangest one I've ever seen pertains to nutrition and happens in my own home. I call it *The Eating-In Problem*. Any time we attempt to prepare a home cooked meal, our kids groan. We've created wonderful dishes, followed recipes line by line, and chosen the best ingredients to emulate restaurant food as closely as we can. And our meals taste better, and are better for you. Nothing seems to matter — to them, eating out is always better.

My kids, like most others, have never seen the inside of any commercial kitchen. They have some sort of unrealistic dream that every kitchen, in every restaurant, is staffed by some broad-shouldered celebrity chef with a bleached-blonde goatee, wearing a pressed apron, a hair net, and a perfect chef's hat. Deep in the recesses of their blessed hearts, they just know that this celebrity chef personally ensures that each and every meal is meticulously cooked, completely from scratch, using only the finest hand-picked, farm-fresh ingredients, in a completely sterile environment.

If Jake's daughter ever realized her tomato soup was cooked by an ex-con who goes by his prison nickname of "Killer," a very scary looking tattoo-laden morbidly obese dude wearing an "I Hate People" t-shirt and a half-torn black hairnet covering the hair he hasn't washed in three days, she might think differently. And if she realized Killer had just emptied another industrial drum of that delicious tomato soup she simply can't get enough of into a poorly washed five-gallon pot as he danced around a family of cockroaches that were scurrying about the kitchen, she might never eat again.

You can surmise why Jake chose to let her go on with her fancy little dream.

Fast forward a few days. Jake, after seeing the longing on his daughter's face as she pined for more of that delicious tomato soup, opened a smaller can of that very same formula in her pristine kitchen. Jake meticulously poured the soup into his very clean stainless steel soup pot. He proceeded to cook it to the perfect temperature for the perfect length of time. Jake then presented a perfectly placed bowl in front of that same daughter. For some unknown reason, daughter made an awful face. She *hated* it. That same daughter said that the same exact soup tasted terrible – *at home.*

But wait, there's more. My own daughter had suddenly developed an aversion to chicken and pasta dishes – but only at home. Yet, she'll boast about how good the pasta dish was at her teenage friend's house or at a restaurant. And whenever she goes out to eat, even with us, what does she order? You guessed it *–chicken or pasta.* And she eats every last bite.

As much your children beat your down, I have absolutely zero doubt that you and all moms and dads are amazing cooks. I'll bet your friends, neighbors, and strangers rave about your dishes. I've gained 15 pounds since we've been married. My husband will even take leftovers for lunch – who does that? Kids must be some sort of freaks. Or, more likely, they're psychologically affected by *The Eating-In Problem.*

Perhaps it's witnessing the *labor* involved in actually preparing a home-cooked meal that discourages or frightens them. Their fragile little minds may be terrified by the thought that they may actually have to remove raw chicken from its frozen packaging, cut the fat off the ends, and spend an hour preparing dinner. God forbid any sort of work takes them away from their social media app of the day.

We all rely upon broad nutritional advice from our government and from physicians, hoping they have at least a small clue about what the average human body requires to remain healthy, and also hoping they are not jaded in some commercially-induced way. What is important to realize is that we are still in the infancy stages of learning how our bodies work, and how nutrition and diet affect us individually. Even the latest or best government or private medical research may be proven wrong, as it has been many times in the past, and will continue to be for quite a while. And now that we have the ability to manipulate genes, we're changing the game before we're completely sure how it worked in the first place. The truth is, collectively, we still don't know the repercussions of changing our food. But there are several questions that can be addressed broadly, and the best research we have thus far on all sorts of nutritional issues is widely available on the internet.

Yet another job you'll have as parent of the year, while building a remarkable resume, is Chief Nutritionist Officer (CNO) of your home. It's your responsibility to introduce nutritious eating habits to your children, and eventually teach them how to acquire the ingredients and skills to prepare those delicious and nutritious meals. You will need to manage their meal times, ensuring they didn't fill up on junk food an hour prior to dinner.

If your child says he or she is full or isn't hungry, don't force them to completely clean their plate, like my parents did. You should serve your children smaller portions to avoid overwhelming them. If they would like more, they'll ask for it. When Josh was about 10, he recalls his mother forcing him to eat some sort of nasty rancid sausage that completely didn't agree with him. Two bites later and Josh managed to destroy her kitchen table and floor with projectile vomit. She learned her lesson. Josh was never forced to eat sausage again. Don't associate mealtime with unnecessary frustration.

At times, children may appear not to eat much at all. Don't worry, they probably won't starve. It's a normal phase of growing up in most cases. Other times, they'll eat like little piglets. Individual dietary needs are dependent on a number of different factors, such as metabolism, age, gender, activity level, and weight. Smaller kids don't require much food – not nearly as much as a full-grown adult does. A couple of bites may often be sufficient to fuel their bodies.

The Food and Drug Administration (FDA) food labeling standard adopts the Recommended Daily Allowances (RDAs) from the average United States Department of Agriculture (USDA) calorie intake dietary guidelines. But the FDA has recently changed a bunch of things that you may remember learning when you were a child. This generation of school kids will learn about a new food pyramid, which is slightly less vague than the old one. It actually gives recommended measured servings rather than simple recommendations. Basically, it's a starting point to achieve what experts consider to be a balanced diet. The new pyramid emphasizes the following:

- *limiting sugar intake*
- *eating more whole grains*
- *avoiding trans fats*
- *limiting saturated fat intake*
- *eating 20% to 35% of daily calories from fats*
- *consuming monounsaturated and polyunsaturated fats*

I began to do a nutritional analysis of my son's eating. In talking with other parents, I found his eating pattern to be typical for his age. One of his dinners, which consisted of four chicken nuggets and about one cup of mashed potatoes topped with brown gravy, plus half cup of milk, consisted of about 473 calories and 1,429 mg of sodium. Add six ounces of pretzel rods for an evening snack, and he definitely exceeded 2,000 mg of sodium for the day, which was well past the recommended 1,500 mg recommended for his age group. I pulled back on the pretzels and offered fruit instead.

I realize that it is increasingly difficult to maintain a balanced diet in our busy lives. We are challenged with processed frozen convenience foods and fast food restaurants at every turn. It takes a concerted effort to purchase and prepare the *right* foods, and an even larger effort to convince your child to eat them. In most cases, you'll need to find a compromise.

Whenever you can, try to avoid processed, packaged, restaurant, and fast foods. Processed foods, like canned soups or frozen dinners, tend to have large amounts of sodium. Many fast food meals are also loaded with sodium. In another flip-flop of nutrition, Monosodium Glutamate (MSG), a flavor enhancer once thought to be harmful, has been determined by several studies to be a safe (and much cheaper) substitute for table salt. With roughly one-third the sodium content, some food geniuses believe it may be healthier to eat foods with MSG than those utilizing traditional salt. If you're concerned about sodium intake, opt for fresh or frozen vegetables instead of the canned variety. Cut back on salty snacks, such as potato chips, nuts, and pretzels and replace them with low-salt or reduced-sodium products.

An important part of a toddler's diet is about 500 mg of calcium per day, which is used primarily for bone growth and proper heart functionality. The best sources of calcium for youngsters are milk and cheese. If your kids are lactose intolerant or don't respond well to dairy products, incorporate calcium-rich foods, including fortified soy products, vegetables, cereals, and calcium enriched orange juice into their diet. It has been determined that toddlers also need 7 mg of iron per day to prevent iron deficiency, which can affect growth, learning, and behavior. Breast-milk contains an easily absorbed type of iron, and baby formula and food is usually iron-fortified. When children switch to people food, it's important to ensure your child is eating good sources of iron including eggs, meats, and fortified cereals.

There are several things you'll want to shy away from. Although not formally proven by the FDA or anyone else to be harmful or disadvantageous, other countries disagree about several foods ingredients and additives. When we're talking about the health of our children, I'd rather err on the side of caution.

The primary offender is high fructose corn syrup (HFCS), a lower cost sweetener found in a surprising array of foods. HCFS is chemically produced from a special type of junk corn grown with federal subsidies. Many people believe HFCS may have something to do with obesity, diabetes, liver disease, and hyperactive attention deficit disorder in children. You'll see this ingredient in nearly every American soda, energy drink, cereal, dessert, and sweetened processed food. The theory is that our bodies don't know how to deal with this type of processed fructose, and it remains in our systems stored as fat. Many Coke addicts search out Coca Cola from Mexico or other countries in ethnic stores because it's still made with real sugar. Personally, I think Mexican Coke tastes better.

You may have heard whispers about the agricultural giant Monsanto quietly lurking in laboratories for decades attempting to create the perfect Frankenstein fruits and vegetables. Their patented inventions are known as genetically modified products (GMO). Many of the fruits and vegetables you'll purchase at your local supermarket have been genetically altered in some manner, naturally (manually spliced while growing on the vine) or artificially (via chemical or DNA manipulation). What's interesting is that these modified foods have been in existence since the early 1990s, and the FDA seemed to automatically consider them all to be safe. But how can you perform long term studies on altered food that you've already approved for mass consumption? We may all be guinea pigs! Corn and soy products are the biggest offenders. And their derivatives (including most sweeteners, corn starch, and MSG) are in virtually everything, from breakfast cereals to tomato sauce. While we're still determining the safety of GMO products, you might want to go as organic as you reasonably can if you have the time and budget. Just in case.

Certain vitamin supplements may not be as good for you as you think. It's always better to get your vitamins and nutrition organically or naturally. An article in the New York Times showed that high concentrations of certain antioxidants have been found to actually increase risk for cancer and other maladies.

Wondering why your kids have a hard time going to sleep? Their little bodies may be fighting to rid themselves of two things they ingested from all that soda they drank that day – HFCS and caffeine. Soda is a bad word in our house. Carbonated water is acidic by nature, causing your body to deviate calcium from your bones and blood in order to maintain a neutral pH level. Considering all the HFCS, caffeine, acids, "secret flavorings," and other craziness laboratories put in soda, you'd think they might be a heartbeat away from poison. Many carbonated energy drinks are much worse, causing reports of heart issues in some children as a result of large amounts of caffeine or certain unproven herbs.

Various sources, some legitimate, others not so much, are beginning to disclose that the fluoride found in most public water taps and in toothpaste may have been used by the Germans to pacify their citizens during World War II. Dentists agree you only need a tiny bit of fluoride for good tooth health, much of which can be found naturally. Confirmed Centers for Disease Control and Prevention (CDC) studies show that excess fluoride can cause bone and tooth damage in small children. There are now warnings in some states that caution parents against using public water supplies with concentrated infant formula. I have a feeling that we're not yet sure what fluoride is doing to the rest of us. Typical water filters found in refrigerators and consumer filters are not effective methods of filtering fluoride. Boiling water can actually *concentrate* fluoride distribution to even higher levels. You'll need something more complex, like reverse osmosis or a distiller, to remove fluoride from your drinking water. Most bottled water is very low on fluoride, unless marked as *fortified with fluoride.*

Food allergies seem so much more common today. Deadly peanut allergies were extremely rare and until the 1990s. My theory is that genetically modified peanuts, bred to incorporate pesticides within the plant itself, are introducing new or modified proteins that some of our bodies recognize as dangerous substances. As a child, I regularly enjoyed fresh fruit, much of which was locally grown. More recently, I cannot eat apples, cherries, plums, pears, or nectarines without developing severe cramps. A physician told me the cause may be the waxy substance that producers use to coat fruit, to make it look shiny in its global transition to market.

Children who are obese are at greater risk from cardiovascular disease, bone and joint problems, sleep apnea, and poor self-esteem, as well as long-term health problems in adulthood. While childhood obesity doesn't always lead to obesity in adulthood, it does raise the risks dramatically. The majority of children who are overweight during preschool or elementary school are still overweight as they enter their teens. Most kids do not outgrow the problem. Addressing weight problems in children requires a coordinated plan of physical activity and healthy nutrition. Never offer dessert as a reward. Withholding dessert sends the message that dessert is the best food, which might increase your child's long-term desire for sweets. Better dessert choices include fresh fruit or yogurt.

There is a dark and potentially deadly side to nutrition. Thanks to all the beautiful skinny people on television and in magazines, some children believe these living Barbie dolls are the norm. Some think that there is something wrong if the mirror does not offer a reflection of that norm. Female adolescents and teens are at a high risk of developing anorexia, bulimia, or binge eating disorders. Keep an eye out for rapid weight loss or a drastic change in eating habits, and consult a physician immediately if you notice anything of this nature.

Making mealtimes fun can mean healthier eating for your kids. You can use creative ways to add more fruit and vegetables to your child's diet with a technique we used to call "fun with food." We'd cut smiley faces in tortillas, create food art or collages using vegetables or fruits, build a mountain and forest with broccoli and mashed potatoes, or make frozen fruit kabobs for the kids.

One more note about dental hygiene. Mr. Twelve Year-Old was very busy with his adventures. He was single-handedly defending his castle, providing moral support for his troops, and disenfranchising those whom dared cross his capitalist pathways. If this little tyrant was in the military, I have no doubt he'd have four stars by the age of sixteen.

We journeyed to the dentist's office one bitterly cold Monday morning in January. As we walked in from the parking lot, I noticed this dentist's office was unusually busy. This guy seemed like the Pied Piper. When I walked into his office, I quickly understood why. You're greeted by a felonious looking white-trash receptionist with a painted-on smile. She hadn't made my acquaintance before, so she looked at me with curious eyes. "New patient?" she asked. Puh-lease. My kid checked himself in and I walked around to explore the office. This guy had two fabulously large salt-water aquariums with the largest overfed Nemos I had ever seen. In the rear of his office, there was a ten by twenty-foot room filled with the greatest arcade games from the twentieth century – all free, and all unlimited play. I didn't want to leave. Ever.

We got called back into the exam area way too quickly. My sixty-pound youngster practically had to pull *me* away from the Ms. Pac Man machine. His office was a maze of brightly colored exam rooms with not-friendly dental hygienists. She attempted to ignore me as I addressed the questions my child snubbed, but that poor soul soon found

I am not one to be ignored. My son sat down and she did her thing. One thing they miss in all dental aide schools is communication skills. You can't ask patients questions while you have a sharp object in their mouth and expect them to answer. Miss Happy finished with her x-rays and announced the dentist would be over shortly. Num-num stayed in the chair and played with the suction straw.

Dr. M finally danced over and pounced on the small rolling stool adjacent to Num-num's exam chair. The dentist asked the same exact standard small-talk questions that he asked to the last four kids. Num-num had his answers ready before he asked, and he spewed them out. I snorted as I failed to hold in my laughter. The doctor was surprised to find my kid had no cavities, and probably wouldn't need braces. I supposed he was distraught he'd get no kickback from the orthodontist this time around. But he did offer some very sound advice – brush those teeth at least twice a day, and for two minutes each time, or he'll be taking his teeth out at night and putting them into the dishwasher.

I had told my kid how important that teeth brushing thing really is, but like most kids, parental advice is always shunned as a nag. However, now that a stranger told him the same exact thing, my advice suddenly became gospel. But that's a blog for another day. Twelve year-olds have no concept of the potential pitfalls of poor dental hygiene. So I painted a picture for him.

My tooth was dead. I had several fillings in that tooth, but the decay was too severe this time and had approached the root. The dentist had no other option other than to refer me to a dental surgeon for a root canal. The root canal itself wasn't that painful, especially with a local anesthetic and nitrous oxide. But the long-term pain of my damaged tooth sucked. It was a constant reminder of my being too busy to properly care for my teeth. I was chewing on Tylenol like candy, and it wasn't helping. During my root canal appointment, the endodontist shoved a large needle into my gums in several locations. "Little pinch." "Another little pinch." "And another." I was about to punch him in his teeth if he punctured my gums one more time. The worst part was that damn rubber dam they placed in my mouth. It's a large sheet of rubber that makes you feel like gagging while it's sitting on the tooth and over your tongue. Once the tooth is numb, they'll begin to drill out the decay. Then, they'll shove a series of relatively large metal files down the tooth into your gums to completely destroy the root and any nerves that may have survived. You can hear and smell the filing. It's particularly nasty. They then will fill the holes they made with some kind of sealer gunk, seal the large hole they made, and eventually place an expensive porcelain crown on top of the rest of the mess.

My kid's eyes kind of glazed over. I think the dentist was about to throw up, or proud that I had broken through my child's imagination with my description. I momentarily wondered if he would add it to his colloquial wordbarf, but quickly realized he wouldn't, because that might adversely affect his revenue stream. The important thing was to convey the moral of the story – that you'd damn well better make time for your teeth, or you'll end up getting jabbed in the mouth with metal objects.

He brushed his teeth twice *and flossed* that night.

26: protecting the flock

Shit happens. It happens a lot. It happens planned, and it happens randomly. And no matter how safe you feel or think you are at a place or in a situation, there's always the possibility that some idiot is going to disturb the peace and change someone's life. As a parent, you need to remain vigilant to protect your ducklings. If and when the time comes, and I hope it never does, for you or for me, you'll instinctively throw yourself in harm's way to protect your children. And that's exactly what you're supposed to do.

Sigmund Freud uncovered that each and every man borders on the fringe of psychotic behavior. Human history and current coordinated efforts labeled as terrorist acts bear witness to this today. Fortunately, most of us get along as we play by the rules of civilization. However, there are those on the fringe of evil. And it's critically important that you, as a parent, can recognize the signs of those on the fringe. There are certain characteristics a woman needs to flush out before making a commitment to a potentially abusive or dangerous relationship. Yes, some women fall into these categories too, but their involvement typically isn't quite as severe or affecting. Whenever you see someone or something that makes you uncomfortable, it's your prerogative to simply avoid it. You don't have to explain yourself, because you're the boss, remember? Change your mind and disallow permission. Postpone your event and go home. Drive somewhere else. Slow down, pull over, and let the possible road rage guy pass you. Take another path. Stay in crowded areas. You can usually tell when something doesn't seem quite right. Follow your intuitions, even if they seem silly, and avoid all avoidable situations. Choose not to become a statistic. It's not a bad idea to explain why you decided to do what you did. Safety and well-being is a very important life lesson.

It's not difficult to end up in a bad situation. Even in the best of neighborhoods, you can't possibly control every external influence in society. We lived in a gated community that was supposed to isolate us from the bad souls in the world. It seemed everything was fine and dandy, until the sweet old couple a few houses down informed us their son was going to stay with them for a while. What they failed to mention was that their little boy was a convicted child molester. You can imagine the ruckus those self-important stay-at-home-moms caused when they caught wind of this development. Someone used a measuring tape to physically measure the distance from the old folks' home to the local children's playground. It was a disastrous mess. We moved out during this craziness, so we weren't able to witness the craziness first hand. Fortunately, we heard the old folks sold their home and moved.

Signs of potential trouble are usually self-evident if you've got your eyes open. In normal everyday situations, a responsible parent is looking for things with the potential to cause harm to their child. I'll routinely scan a restaurant or bar for people who simply look angry. I will also scan public places, shopping malls and parking lots for kids or adults who look like they're up to no good.

Keep your finger on the pulse of your child's social life. Know their friends. Meet their parents to see what they're all about. Don't be afraid to listen to your inner voice and pass judgment when necessary. Prevention of a problem is always better than attempting to remedy a bad situation. Remember, it's your primary function to protect and guide your children in an effort to help them become responsible, law-abiding adults. Society doesn't work if we don't all follow the rules. Some folks haven't received that memo.

There are several obvious and readily available indicators you will immediately notice that indicate bad judgment. Learn to look for them, and teach your children about these indicators too. You can disagree all you want, tattoo boy with the loud-ass low-rider with spinners, but you'll see – once you kick into full parenthood mode.

The Booming System. There is no good reason to have subwoofers in your automobile providing enough decibels to permanently damage your hearing. And the fact that you willingly and purposefully want to annoy everyone outside your car leads me to believe you are disrespectful. The awful thoughtless music selection that accompanies this kind of silliness is the second strike. Third strike? Someone, probably a parent, paid several hundred bucks to facilitate this stupidity. You've just given me indisputable evidence of purely bad judgment, which is also distributed throughout your entire gene pool. Please keep your vehicle out of my hood, and stay away from my children. I hope you enjoy your dishwashing career. Too bad that will be automated soon.

Oversized chrome wheels or "spinners." If you're so vain that you felt the need to spend two to four thousand dollars to buy or rent 20-inch chrome rims and new high-performance tires for a 20 year-old rusted out vehicle that barely runs, I can imagine the other poor choices you're going to make in life. You could have saved or invested that money, or donated it to a worthwhile charity. Those pricey ghetto wheels have absolutely nothing to do with the performance or fuel economy of your vehicle. You've proved that you are a vain person with little common sense.

Low-riders. It's difficult to have worse judgment than spinners, but someone with a low-rider definitely wins that battle. Why anyone in their right mind would want to spend thousands of dollars to make their stock automobile more susceptible to speed bumps, curbs, road hazards, and puddles is beyond me. Do you actually think your low rider and bad tattoos will get you more booty? Additionally, lowering your vehicle obviously lowers your carefully engineered safety standards and makes you more susceptible to bodily harm in the event of an accident. Definitely don't want my children palling around with these low-intelligence idiots.

Pick-up trucks. Most people who drive pick-up trucks will never pick up anything. Now that country music stars are mainstream, their silly lyrics have immortalized this useless vehicle as a trademark of their style. Truck dealers are laughing all the way to the bank as you drive off their lots in overpriced hick vehicles (upwards of $45,000) with inconvenient uncovered storage areas. If you're not a tradesman carrying tools or dirt in the back of your truck, then you're an easily influenced flighty moron. I've heard stories of children riding in the back of these trucks and dying after being ejected after a quick turn or hard bump. And who knows what other kind of stupidity someone could talk you into.

Crotch Rockets. In New York, if you own a sporty motorcycle, you're now invited to be part of a gang of idiots who do tricks on public freeways, threatening the safety of law-abiding citizens. One not-so-smart young man found out the hard way that stopping short in front of a frightened man and his family in an SUV was a bad idea. I would have ran his ass over too. Unfortunately, this trend of youngsters congregating on their sporty motorcycles is gaining national momentum. It's important to realize that there is a big difference between "bikers" and idiots. Bikers are usually 50 years-old or older, are gainfully employed, and they ride with respect. But if you're dealing with a young'un who has a bike, and it ain't a Harley, you might want to think about pouring a pound of sugar in his gas tank and slashing his tires before you let this fool go out with your daughter.

Ties. I used to think it was a pure coincidence that the word *ties* rhymed with *lies*. Today I'm not so sure. If you think about who generally wears ties in today's informal society, you'll quickly realize it's mostly sales-folk. And *sales* is generally synonymous with *deceit*. He who tells the biggest tale, tends to get the biggest sale. A tie is a quick and surefire way to recognize a sociopath. As an aside, a bowtie is an easy way to recognize a waiter, a stripper, a brilliant scientist, or a fucking hipster.

Moustaches. There is only one profession remaining in our world that seems to endorse lip hair, and that's your local police. There is no legitimate explanation, rhyme, or reason why so many cops have moustaches. It may be some secret rite of passage. I've asked several cops, but they're all tight lipped (pun intended) about the whole thing. If your child's buddy has a moustache and he is not a cop, that's a definite red flag. Other facial hair may be troubling, too. Especially those cleverly shaped goatees or

Abraham Lincoln sideburns. These kids are insecure and desperately seeking attention through their facial hair. Proceed with caution.

Shaved heads. Especially with anyone who is not African-American. Back in the day, Marvin Lewis, a cleanly shaven black man, and I had a long discussion about why many black men shave their heads. And I have to admit, if I had to exercise that much maintenance on my hair, I'd shave my head too. Unless you're active duty military, or have a lice problem, there's no real reason to shave your head. But many white guys and Hispanics shave their heads to look gangsta, or worse, like skinheads who represent the Arian Nation. And both of those reasons are equally poor; both representing an extremely negative statement rather than simple hygiene. When you look into the eyes of someone who has shaved his head, I'll bet you too will see nothing. No one's home. No aspirations. No empathy. And definitely no contact with my sons or daughters, thank you. Oh, one more thing – shaved head guys typically wear baseball caps to hide their lack of hair. And rednecks wear baseball caps too, but that's because they're too lazy to wash their hair. I make kids take their hats off in my house, just to check.

Here are some other scary and dangerous types of people you don't want to get involved with, individually, or as a family.

The Fighting Man. An older gentleman, in an attempt to make small talk, asked me what my hobbies were. I replied that my hobbies were diverse and unique. He aptly considered me a *complicated person.* In turn, I posed the same question to him. The man replied that he's into boxing and UFC – Ultimate Fighting for those of you who aren't familiar with that sport. I had to look it up too. In my best southern drawl, I asked him if he garnered pleasure from the act of two people beating the piss out of each other. He replied that he enjoyed a good fight, having been an active boxer in a previous life. A man who takes pleasure in harming another man is more of a warrior than a civilized human being. He has stepped over the bounds of repressing his desire to harm in the guise of a terrible error in judgment which ultimately led to socially acceptable behavior. Despite his clever disguise as nothing more than a big teddy bear, be aware that his inner warrior lurks and could be aroused with little or no warning.

The Hunting Man. As little as 100 years ago, before butchers, general stores, supermarkets, Walmart, and food stamps, it was more necessary for man to hunt to feed himself and his family. Today, hunting exists as sport only. As I ponder this "sport," I wonder what the real challenge and acquisition is. There is no battle, as we use an increasing amount of power and technology to overcome an otherwise helpless and usually innocent animal, be that fish, fowl, deer, or bear. If you've ever tried venison, you'll agree that it's a forced taste – particularly chewy with a strange bitter flavor. Regardless of their excuse, a hunter means to show his masculinity by killing an animal and bragging to his friends. Remember, these man have a cadre of deadly weapons at their immediate disposal. The worst offenders are those who employ the services of a taxidermist.

The Sports Fan. Sports are a wonderful way to exercise and release tension, especially in a participatory or coaching role. However, a man who is broadly into two or more sports as a spectator is on the other side of this spectrum. Subjectively, I have found that a man's mood and attitude can be directly affected by the performance of a collegiate or professional sports team. Frankly, that level of influence is disturbing. This indicates a narcissistic tendency which is projected through his financial investment in branded merchandise or memorabilia. Your relationship, family, and feelings will, at times, be relegated to the cheap seats.

The Overly Religious Bro. In the absence of complete brainwashing as a child, which is evident in radical religious sects worldwide, adults turn to religion when something they value is missing in their lives. Love, money, health, status, or several other characteristics can drive a person to become a religious zealot. Once a person eschews the reality of the world you live in and decides things might be better on the other side, his behavior can become quite questionable. If quotations from his favorite book are a predominant part of his everyday conversation, you may want to have a discussion before you get seriously involved.

The Gangsta. Finally, any man who idolizes criminal activity, through music, movies, or in real life, has an innate desire to emulate his heroes. Sooner or later, he will act on that desire, and his naive and amateur actions could prove devastating to his life, career, and relationships. It is critically important to be firmly grounded in reality for any relationship to be successful.

My daughters are active in the dating world. I attempted to steer them towards becoming lesbians by ensuring them I am a tolerant hipster, but that didn't work out. I figured lesbian daughters might stave off my becoming a grandparent prematurely. But I am more concerned about broken hearts, and more so, broken dreams. I have seen one too many failed relationships that have taken a brutal toll on formerly happy people, permanently inserting a fork in their road of life that headed in the wrong direction. Any responsible parent should attempt to protect his children from such a fate.

From my years of experience in dating, being dated, and observing others, here are the five men you and your daughters would be better off avoiding. Of course, there are exceptions to every rule. But those exceptions are quite rare. Don't fall into that endless chasm of hope that blinds your reality.

Tattoos are permanent (and painful) damage to the largest organ on your body, your skin. I'm not talking about the ex-Green Beret who proudly displays his unit on a now faded obscure tattoo on his upper arm. I'm talking the brother with the complete sleeve tattoos, on both arms, and now the front and back of his neck. If you're not in that underworld, a pro tat studio charges upwards of $500 for one single two to three-inch single-color segment on an arm. Count up all the five-spots, and these fools have spent upwards of $5,000 permanently defacing their bodies. Crazy tattoo people are anti-establishment, i.e., anti-civilization. They have given up trying to fit in to society, knowing damn well that a business suit will fail to hide their "art." Obviously, this will permanently limit their earning ability, which leads to housing in less-desirable areas, which leads to less-desirable schools, and I'm sure you can imagine how that typically ends up. Be especially aware of face tattoos, which indicate a certain type of mental situation. And learn to recognize gang and prison tattoos for a whole other bunch of warning signs. A small, obscure, hidden tattoo that I should never be aware of – although still an obvious indication of faulty judgment – isn't necessarily a deal breaker.

The Smoker. It's common knowledge that smoking (anything) is most likely bad for your health. A good indication of common sense might be that someone avoids smoking altogether until a final consensus is reached. Also, now that a pack of cigarettes is about five or six bucks, that's a pricey habit for a fairly mediocre and temporary nicotine high. Vapes are even worse. Most people begin smoking because they think it looks cool, and that should be the first sign of trouble – an insecurity complex. Insecure people do strange and unpredictable things, like harder drugs and having sex with risky people.

Oh – and if he or she used the "medicinal purposes" excuse, you might want to look up a notice from the United States Attorney General which states that excuse is typically a bunch of hooey.

The Shaver. The easiest indication of an apparent narcissist, these fools shave their beards or moustaches into strangely unnatural alien configurations. It takes a lot of time to groom yourself, which is usually a good thing. But the fact that a man feels the need to shave his beard into a perfectly shaped pattern indicates he's looking to attract attention usually from the opposite sex. He thinks he's daring and masculine with his wannabe model looks. While a normal guy lets his beard grow naturally, or a man lets his facial hair grow a couple days into a natural scruff, this brother is on a mission. And it's usually not a good mission for you or your daughters.

The other end of this spectrum is the non-shaver. A man who lets his beard grow into a Muslim-looking mess is either lazy or fundamentally religious, both of which are deal breakers in my book.

The Bodybuilder. There's an obvious difference between fitness and narcissism. Think a bicycle rider versus a weight lifter. The bike rider is getting cardiovascular exercise, seeing some sights, breathing in fresh air, and actually going somewhere. But a weightlifter is working on that six-pack and Popeye arms for another reason – *vanity*. He's attempting to look buff for a reason – to attract compliments from his weight-lifting homies, or to pick up narrow-minded women with a low IQ. Sure, as discussed previously, women are wired to search for a man who they think will protect them and their offspring. And no doubt these guys are nice to look at. The problem is the situation is almost always *temporary*. As you get a little older and begin to look your age, he's off to his next conquest, and that means you (and your children) will be left alone – and unprotected. And eventually, his pretty body mass turns to fat.

This is just a brief sampling of characteristics and personality traits you'll need to watch for and teach your sons and daughters to avoid for their own safety and well-being. It's all about bad judgment. Most youthful bad judgment stems from insecurity. Insecurity breeds poor choices and instability. I don't want that for my daughters, and you shouldn't want that for yourselves either.

Teens have an invulnerability complex. They've fallen off bikes and swings, bumped their heads a bunch of times, and probably survived a fight or two, and they're still here. *Party!* Society does a terrible job of teaching kids that our bodies, and life in general, are fairly fragile. Kids aren't watching the news – they're watching sitcoms where every situation meets a neat and tidy ending every thirty minutes. The real world doesn't work that way, and it's your responsibility to convey that lesson.

By keeping abreast of situations, trends, and events that might not be the best thing for your child, you should be able to have several attractive distractions at your disposal when you need them. They don't have to be elaborate or costly, just cool enough to create a diversion that won't make missing that keg party seem so horrible. I'm not going to lie – it's hard to find fun things to do. What's important is not to have done everything before the kid turns twelve.

Divorced moms can be kind of squirrely, especially this one who we'll call Sandy. Since Sandy had no man in her life, she decided she was going to spoil her son. By the ripe-old age of 12, he was tired of fishing, bored with paintball, shot with shooting, finished with most video games, hated all sports, and didn't want to learn any musical instruments. This kid has been all over Florida, New York, Las Vegas, the Grand Canyon, skiing, and on countless cruises. He's now at a point where he refuses to go on any "old" cruise ships, and avoids the entire Carnival fleet, because they're simply not up to his standards. He's already seen Blue Man, La Nouba, Wicked, and several Broadway shows. He lives just outside of Orlando, so Disney, Universal, Lego Land,

and Wet and Wild are all old to him, too. When the boy's dad picks him up for his week, he has no idea what to do with this kid. There was nothing left.

Space your activities out, especially if you're a divorced parent. Please. It won't kill him or her to spend a weekend at home being bored with the family once in a while. You could talk. Play board games. Play hide and seek. Draw something. Do crafts. Stare at each other. *Anything.*

One of our girls was hanging out with a group who had a little too much freedom. We were talking to one of the moms at a football game about drinking, and that silly woman remarked, "Oh, it's not so bad if they have a drink or two as long as they're home. We did, and we're still here." *Really?* Your daughter is *fourteen*, you idiot! We immediately blacklisted that mom, her daughter, and any parties at her home. A few weeks later, it was this chick's birthday. Our daughter wanted to go because, of course, *everyone* was going to be there. She cried and begged us for permission to go. We came up with a story that we had planned a weekend getaway at a resort hotel weeks ago, and we couldn't cancel the reservations without losing our money. She was disappointed, but the distraction worked. She had fun at the hotel. We later heard several hundred uninvited guests crashed the party, started fights, and the police showed up to shut it down early.

Here are some other distractions you may find helpful when closing the door on a potentially bad situation.

- *Church retreats*
- *Theatre or other similar shows*
- *Indoor or outdoor rock climbing or zip lines*
- *Bike riding, hiking, or walking around a park or nature trail*

- *Tennis, Basketball, Soccer, Football, Swimming, or any other sport*
- *Scrabble, Sorry, Trouble, cards, or other board games*
- *Exploring a hotel or other publicly accessible place*
- *Camping*
- *Cruises*
- *Scavenger hunts*
- *Weekend*   *getaways.*

27: fairytales

No offense intended, but this chapter will undoubtedly offend everyone. Whenever you discuss religion, without fail, someone always gets pissed off. If you want the truth, continue reading. If not, please skip to the next chapter.

If you have ever asked any devout Christian about Jesus, you'll most certainly elicit a wide and cheeky smile as he or she becomes enthralled in sharing years of brainwashing with you. Their faces light up, because they have no worries in the world. Devout Christians have been completely convinced that this life is largely irrelevant – it's nothing more than a temporary ride towards a perfect eternal existence. In their wide glassed-over eyes, nothing really matters. Apathy is encouraged and completely acceptable, due to all the clever workarounds their convenient little story provides. You know, free will, mysterious ways, he has a plan, et cetera.

But what really strikes me, about Christians in particular, is how goddamned *happy* they seem to be. If ignorance is bliss, it certainly looks much more attractive than the truth. Unfortunately, for me, Morpheus convinced me to take the red pill (see *The Matrix*).

Two thousand years ago, some bearded, blonde-haired, blue-eyed, All-American looking Jewish Middle-Eastern bro took all the worry and fear out of everything. Today, thanks to Mr. Christ, Christians can do whatever they want (as long as they apologize) and they've earned a ticket for some invisible escalator going to a wonderful fluffy place with pearly gates that they call Heaven. And you get to hang out there, with all your dead relatives, and every other person who ever died, plus the big guy himself, for all eternity. I have to admit, it all sounds pretty awesome. And with literally *billions* of fellow believers all patting you on the back, it's quite easy to fall in line with this belief. It's attractive. It's easy.

The downfall of religion is that we're all stuck on this planet with billions of careless people on autopilot who firmly believe in various fairy tales with no incentive to make our collective life on this planet any better. Sure, they'll all go on their little retreats and occasional "mission" trips to help people in need. But what they're really doing is bribing folks and attempting to convert them to Christianity by handing out bibles, or in some extreme religions, suicide bombs.

Historians have cataloged well over 2,000 gods. Count the Hindu beliefs about the universe, and you can then inflate the god bubble to well over 300 *million*. So which God is the "right" one? Which god is the *real* one? We've been hurling insults and killing each other over this question for millennia. When you really think about it logically, the overwhelming probability is that we're *all* wrong, and there may be no single god at all. And I will personally guarantee that if there is a single boss God, he probably isn't a white male who looks strikingly like James Franco, Morgan Freeman, or one of your redneck neighbors. In the unlikely event that God happens to be humanoid, he probably looks more like Shaq. And considered where and when he was born, Jesus probably looked a little more like Saddam Hussein than any Caucasian Hollywood actor.

Going to church is kind of like going to the movies. Only it's the same script, week after week, year after year, and it hasn't really changed for the past two thousand years. Since civilization was created long before the internet, different folks in different parts of the world created several varied religions with many different stories. Even Christianity itself is split into thousands of denominations. Some cultish weirdo who lives on my block has his own flavor, and jams up my street every Wednesday night preaching his silliness. What's crazy is, he'll let his three year old daughter out on to the street, alone, in the dark, while his in-home church meeting is held. I quietly keep an eye out for her when I can. I'm pretty sure God didn't sanction abandoning your parental duties.

Many organized religions have repeatedly plagiarized the same exact story about the son, a virgin birth, an execution and subsequent resurrection, and the promise of an eventual return of some deity to pronounce some kind of fiery judgment. Over time, they've all changed a few names and details to make it a bit more personal. Yet millions of people will devote their time, energy, reputation, savings, and even their lives to support the institution that brainwashed them first. That's some holding power: to tell the same story for two thousand years, promising a glorious end nicknamed "salvation" (that's always coming soon) – and keep people coming back, not to mention keeping them paying.

Perhaps the best question to ask is "why is there religion?" Humans are inherently weak. Many of us are kind of lost. We are the only species of animal that we are aware of whose consciousness enables us to wonder *why* we are here. Consequently, this ability makes us fear what will happen when we're done with this bag of bones we call a body. Religion was created, by us, to fill our emptiness. Organized religion is a very effective play on fear, and religious leaders are very aware of that. Many people believe that religion was created by the wealthy, providing them with an excuse as to why they were *chosen* to be rich, and you weren't. I have to admit, that is a very plausible theory. The lord works in mysterious ways.

One of the most ironic (and comical) things you can do is sit somewhere in a church parking lot immediately after any service, and watch parishioners drive rudely and even flip people off as they all make a mad rush for the exits. No matter how many thank yous and forgive mes and peace-be-with-yous your fellow parishioners shared in mass, they have all been forgotten the moment they walk out the door. My moment of awakening occurred as I was leaving a Catholic church in New Jersey one Sunday morning. I witnessed a small fender-bender in the church parking lot, as people were rushing out to get ready for a football game. There was chaotic screaming and fisticuffs that ensued afterwards. The police were summoned to break it up. Peace be with you? I think not. I never went back to that church again.

Religion does have a purpose in a civilized society. Today, we aren't permitted to remove weak minded people from our gene pool. But if those weak minded people weren't afraid of going to Hell, just imagine the criminal chaos they'd cause for the rest of us. It's a necessary civilized control that has both worked wonders and perpetrated atrocities throughout man's adolescence. Actually, religion in youth can prove to be a wonderful control. You can keep your children in a comfortable and safe little clique and minimize outside influences to build a solid foundation with less of a societal attitude and a more receptive environment for learning.

Ironically, in Christianity, all you have to do is admit your sin, apologize, and you're off the hook. Buddhism doesn't seem to care what you do. But other religions aren't quite as tolerant. Although pure Islam is portrayed as a peaceful religion, radical Islam is a dangerous faction. Cutting off someone's hand for shoplifting is quite an effective deterrent, but it's a bit severe. I have seen one of my friend's weak-minded sisters convert to this religion. In my eyes, since she is a woman, she is misguided and mistreated. But even in her misery, this small-minded woman believes she is happy.

If you choose to avoid the institutions, you'll still need to handle the religion subject at some point. Depending on your child's age, religious discussions always get kind of sketchy. You'll field questions like, why are we here? Why are there religious wars? Why are there so many different Gods? What happens after we die? Why didn't God save that little kid from being killed? Why did God create Ebola? I explain that none of us know the answers to any of those questions. Your replies need to be tailored to their age and level of maturity, or your children may never fall asleep again. I tell my children that I don't know where we're from, but logically, we have to be from somewhere. Although objectivity is very important, it is equally important not to abandon hope, and not to criticize whatever religious beliefs your children may develop, unless they're the dangerous or obscenely peculiar ones. When pressed, I tell my children something like:

I do believe in miracles. The fact that we're living, breathing, and talking right now are all miracles. An orange grown from a seed into a tree that somehow knows how to consistently make perfect oranges is a miracle. You too, a perfect being, were born from a seed in my womb, and you are a miracle.

Life is so complex, so mysterious, and so miraculous that it would be pompous for humanity to believe they could begin to understand who or what created our universe, or more importantly, *why*. If we are to survive as a species, the most important thing any parent should teach their children is *tolerance*. We will never achieve world peace unless we can all collectively agree that we really don't know anything about anything.

No one can advise you how to handle religion as a parent, because that is a very personal choice. Handle it the best way you know how. Like parenting, religion is imperfect at best. Your mileage and faith may vary.

28: the law

It continually amazes me what a poor job our school systems do teaching our children about basic societal functionality. Two of our children graduated from different high schools in different states four years apart, and neither had the knowledge how to write a check or address an envelope. However, they both were forced to memorize the capital of Iowa, wrote literary papers on the author's intent in writing Catcher in the Rye, and can recite the quadratic formula backwards. Granted, the check writing and letter addressing skills are quickly becoming obsolete in the age of online bill paying, but they still remain critical adult life skills.

What is not obsolete are your rights as an American citizen. Although students were hopefully introduced to The Constitution and the Bill of Rights during elementary school, their applicable knowledge of these documents, recent judicial interpretations, and their relevant purpose in our society is surprisingly limited. If your kids haven't watched fictional crime shows on network television, they may have no idea of the inalienable rights they possess in the eyes of the law. This educational responsibility will be yours as a parent. Unfortunately, you might not have the 411 either if you went through the same shoddy educational system a generation or two earlier.

The "Patriot Act" and its subsequent ripple effects have blurred many of your inherent rights. Was that necessary? Probably, in many ways, to keep us safe. But stick to your guns (yet another pun intended). Evidence in non-terrorist cases will probably be ruled as inadmissible if recovered during inappropriate or illegal search and seizures. So don't be a terrorist. And tell your children don't even joke about terrorism. Surveillance sweeps far and wide, social media is easy to uncover, and there's no sense of humor at Homeland Security or the Department of Justice.

I am not an attorney, so technically, I cannot give anyone legal advice. A good friend of mine, who is an attorney, provided some wonderfully generic non-legal advice that you hopefully will never need, but may find interesting and helpful.

Although there are thousands of laws the average person may never be aware of, you or your child can never use ignorance of the law as a defense unless you are judged mentally incompetent, which ironically is insanely difficult to prove. Your best bet is to teach your children to use common sense and not to do anything you, they, or any reasonable person might consider morally wrong. Lawyers are very expensive, court appearances are inconvenient, and your name and mugshot shown on a website or in a newspaper is generally not a good thing. In today's salacious society, regardless of your guilt or the outcome of your trial, upon you or your child's arrest for anything, you can be sure all your local tabloids will post your mug shot on their website or in their newspaper effectively rendering your reputation *guilty until proven innocent*. People get fired from good jobs, disowned by families, and could lose valuable opportunities in the future due to a permanently tarnished reputation. Unfortunate circumstances can plague both good and bad people, for a plethora of good and bad reasons. So try like hell to never get arrested.

There are a few common sense Civil Liberty rights every American should be aware of. Here's what you should tell your children.

You have a right to remain silent. I'm sure you've heard this in movies and on television – they call it *taking the fifth*, which is technically invoking protection afforded to you by the fifth amendment of the United States Constitution, which was created to help alleviate self-incrimination. You cannot be arrested or charged for refusing to answer questions. Anything you do say to anyone while in police custody can and will be used against you in a court of law. If you are ever arrested, *politely* tell the officer you are aware of this right and you choose to invoke it, and you'd like to speak with an attorney just in case. Some officers might get chummy with you and tell you it's not necessary, but it absolutely is. More importantly. don't be a cocky or belligerent jerk, or you might get your ass beaten badly if you happen to tangle with the wrong policeman (your race and his race won't matter – there are bad eggs across all races). You deserve to be treated with respect, and so does the officer of the law. What's important to realize is that the police person is doing his or her job. And it can be a really shitty job. Everyone has bad days, and everyone has a breaking point. Don't set yourself up to take a beating you don't deserve.

Depending an officer's judgment, mood, or morality, you could also be arrested for something you *didn't* do. Contrary to popular belief, you don't have to be told what you've been arrested for until you're at the police station being booked. And an officer does *not* have to read your *Miranda* rights, the list of rights you have as an accused person, until they have decided to formally question you. It's all a bit confusing, especially when in the stressful situation of being detained. It's best to always *respectfully* decline answering anything until you have consulted with an attorney. Let your attorney set things straight, whether you are guilty or not. Your Miranda rights are as follows:

- *You have the right to remain silent.*
- *Anything you say or do may be used against you in a court of law. That may include your actions, gestures, Tweets or Instagram posts.*
- *You have the right to consult an attorney before speaking to the police and to have an attorney present during questioning, now or in the future.*
- *If you cannot afford an attorney, one will be appointed for you before any questioning, but only if you request one.*
- *If you decide to answer any questions now, without an attorney present, you always have the right to stop answering at any time if you decide you want to talk to an attorney.*
- *Knowing and understanding your rights as the law enforcement officer has explained them to you, police may still ask you to answer questions without an attorney present. Just don't.*

Call an attorney, even if you can't afford one – a public defender will be provided for you free of charge. Those attorneys aren't necessarily the best attorneys – they're typically new or fresh out of law school, so they may not have the experience and contacts you need for a solid defense. And more aggressive PDs may be trying to impress defense attorneys and judges in an effort to secure a much more lucrative job on the other side of the aisle. But, it's better than no attorney at all.

Technically, you do have the right to free speech. But there are several things your children cannot or should not say, text, email, post, Tweet, or write on Facebook. Assume that anything you type on the Internet is permanent. Screenshots are easy to capture, deleted items are never really deleted, and all kinds of things you'd never think of are often admissible in court.

Although you do have freedom of speech, it can cost you. If you make false statements about people or companies, you can be sued for damages. And, non-celebrity citizens (like your ex-boyfriends) are entitled to a certain level of privacy. Even if your malicious statements are true, you could be sued for defamation of character. In cases of libel (written or electronic defamatory statements) or slander (spoken statements) you've written or said against a company or person, the burden of proof will fall upon you, which can be expensive and inconvenient. And your employer may have the right to fire you based on what you've said. Teach your children that silence is golden.

Although you, as an adult, can legally possess dirty magazines and videos, you (or your children) cannot possess or distribute any sort of sexually explicit or even suggestive photos or videos featuring anyone who may be under the age of 18. If you're not sure, don't possess it. *Make sure your children (and their friends) are aware of this.* If something inappropriate was downloaded or shared on a computer that you, the parent, technically own, and it's done via the internet connection you're paying for, guess who the FBI is going to come knocking for?

Obscenity, threat of bodily harm, hate speech, and fighting words may be construed as criminal, depending on their phrasing and the jurisdiction you fall under. And any threat that could be construed as "terrorist", which is now covered by a very large umbrella, joking or not, will get you imprisoned quickly. Tell your children to think carefully about what they're going to say before they say it. It's a great life rule.

Although it's technically a constitutional privilege, your right to privacy is subject to a very loose interpretation. Assume anyone and everyone might find out about everything you do, so lean towards doing the right thing. But you do have rights against people poking their eyes, ears, and hands where they don't belong. Technically, you don't have to let anyone search you, your car, or your home without a warrant. Although clever badge-holding pundits may pull the probable cause or Patriot Act cards, most criminal defense lawyers will tell you, off the record, to attempt to deny that search anyway – especially if you *do* have something to hide. It's much more difficult to establish *admissible* evidence (evidence than may be used in court by a judge or jury to convict someone) from a questionable search. If your child is home alone and under 18, they never have to open the door for *anyone*, unless there's an obvious emergency.

Bad people impersonate cops. Anyone can buy emergency lights and fake badges on websites like eBay, and it is very difficult to tell what's real – and especially when you're in a situation of surprise. If you know for a fact that you haven't done anything wrong, but you're being pulled over by an unmarked car and the officer does not have a proper uniform, keep your windows up and doors locked, put your flashers on, drive a little further, and wait to pull over in a well-lit area with lots of people around if possible. Roll down your window, just enough for him to hear you, and ask for identification. Actually LOOK at the ID, make a note of his first and last name, and tell him you would like to call 911 to verify he is a *real* officer before opening your window or door all the way.

He shouldn't have any problem with this. If he's a fake, he'll hopefully leave immediately. If he doesn't, you're already on the phone with a 911 dispatcher. Once you're confident that he or she is for real, you'd better roll down your window, or he might break it.

A well-regulated militia being necessary to the security of a free state, the right of the people to keep and bear arms shall not be infringed. That poorly written, barely literate statement has been bastardized into the right for anyone to own as many guns as she wants. That doesn't mean you have the inherent right to *carry* a gun with you wherever you go. Most jurisdictions require a federal background check and a special permit for you to actually carry a concealed (hidden) gun on your person. Although it might look cool in the movies to shove a Glock down the back of your pants, that act is quite illegal in most places, and can be a felony. And many "gangstas" have accidentally shot their own private parts. I imagine that hurts physically, and mentally. So please, advise your children not to carry weapons, even if you're a card-carrying NRA member.

Finally, you are legally protected against discrimination. You cannot be denied education, employment, housing, or voting rights based on your gender, race, creed, color, religion, or sexual orientation. You probably can, however, be denied employment (and given dirty looks) because you have pink hair, offensive tattoos, wide gaping holes in your ear lobes, or a piece of metal inconveniently shoved through the bottom of your nose. And unless your kid is interviewing with Chris Christie, they should be taught to never wear a Dallas Cowboys jersey to a job interview anywhere around Philadelphia, because that's just plain wrong.

There are certain things you cannot do in the eyes of the law. Obviously, theft, murder, vandalism, and other things that trigger a normal person's moral compass should be avoided. But there are many grey areas, including fraud, extortion, hacking, price gouging, and certain things you cannot (and should not) do at certain ages. One of the most confusing areas deals with something called statutory rape. States establish their own arbitrary age at which they consider a minor child old enough or mature enough to engage into consensual sexual relations. For example, in Florida, an 18-year-old student was in a consensual sexual relationship with a 14-year-old girl who also attended her school. The 18-year-old was arrested for statutory rape, because Florida's state statutes establish that a 14-year-old girl was not mature enough to make her own decisions about sex. Depending on where you live, even "first base" can be considered rape. In Florida, "a person who intentionally touches, in a lewd or lascivious manner, the breasts, genitals, genital area, or buttocks, *or the clothing covering them*, of a person less than 16 years of age, or forces or entices a person under 16 years of age to touch the perpetrator, commits lewd or lascivious molestation." And that's a *felony*, kids.

Where it gets weird is if the victim was 16 at the time of their sexual relationship, everything might have been okay. In Florida, a 16-year-old can legally have sex with someone who's up to 23 years old. But, if that same 16-year-old had birthday sex with that same person on his or her 24th birthday, the 24-year-old would be charged with statutory rape. It makes my head spin too.

The perpetrator's ignorance of the victim's age, and surprisingly the victim's *misrepresentation* of his or her age cannot be used as a defense in a prosecution under many state laws. So your child had better be an expert at carbon dating and tooth records; otherwise have him or her ask for an embossed birth certificate, two forms of government-issued photo identification, plus a notarized letter – all, of course, in the heat of the moment.

Each state has their own "age of consent," which is as low as 16 in several states. You can usually find this information online on your state's website. Of course, it's always safer to consult an attorney.

There are enough variables in law to make your head spin. You must make your children aware of these laws, and caution them against breaking them to avoid legal issues and social suicide. Your best bet is to tell your children they're not allowed to date until they're at least 16 years old, and their partners must be at least 16 and less than 21. As a responsible parent, you'll always know where your children are, so they can't possibly engage in such behavior, right?

If you get arrested while still actively parenting, regardless of your guilt or the charge, you'd better pack it in and move your family to another state. You'll be blacklisted on everything within 24 hours. Bad news spreads at the speed of light.

And it's important to let your children know the same goes for them. One little run in with local, state, or federal law, and their mugshot will be splashed on every Facebook community and Instagram account for 200 square miles.

Although this policy sucks for the innocent, it can be beneficial at times. It doesn't hurt to do a quick background check on your kid's peers and even their parents before getting involved in potentially compromising situations, like dating, sleepovers, combined family vacations, or binding financial contracts. Chances are they've probably already run one on you.

29: it's all about the benjamins

Kim Kardashian and her equally talented sisters earned more than $60 million dollars in 2015. And no one is quite clear on what they actually do. I suppose someone has to pay for Caitlyn Jenner's estrogen shots. Although Jenner hasn't been on a Wheaties box in decades, he still earns his own millions. In 2014, Kim's ex-husband Kris Humphries banked over $4 million for bouncing a small orange ball around a court and missing the net more than he made it. But the Kardashians aren't the only ones banking megabucks – even that nerdy DJ Ryan Seacrest pocketed about $15 million for uttering a few, occasional, unimportant words, during another floundering season of American Idol. It seems society likes to throw crazy money at certain people for doing unimportant things.

Our culture is the reason for the season. Your children will be inundated with marketing messages from the moment they can first focus their eyeballs. As we've already discussed, our popular culture portrays everyone as wealthy. Peer pressure compounds the desire of non-wealthy children to have what their peers have. The entitled-society fight is one you can't possibly win. But what you can do is set a strong foundation in reality, and in money management.

At first glance, it sure seems like it is not too difficult to be wealthy in America. After all, a whole lot of no-talent people who aren't too much different than you and me are multi-millionaires. So it must be easy to get swagger, right? *Wrong.* Statistically, unless you've made a really good sex tape, you've got a better chance of being hit by lightning. Better saddle up with your more modest companions in that vanishing middle-class neighborhood, because chances are, that's where you too will end up.

Regardless of your socioeconomic status, money is a finite resource. There's only so much to go around, and everyone who has it is very stingy with it – especially those who are fortunate enough to have a lot. It is a well-known fact that most wealthy people are terrible tippers. And ironically, they have the confidence and wherewithal to haggle about everything, spending less than those who don't have enough. As a business person, I have witnessed this on several occasions. But I don't let the bastards get away with it. The late great Davis Brown once told me, "Sell to the classes, eat with the masses. But sell to the masses, eat with the classes." I'm not sure if his words were bastardized or where he picked ditty that up, but it's a doozy.

Your children will need money to survive. If they want some money to fulfill their needs and wants, they'll need to beg, borrow, steal, or more likely, *earn* it. But our entitled youth believes that the world can be theirs with nothing more than a swipe of plastic. Unreasonable and often debilitating levels of consumer debt are now widely accepted and recognized as the new norm. You can effortlessly borrow as much as you want, and you can easily live well beyond your means. But you will be expected to pay interest payments (that often exceed the cost of your original purchase) on your line of credit for the rest of your life.

My children all had a stunning revelation when I taught them minimum wage is about eight bucks an hour. That seems like a whole lot of cash to a kid, until they begin to do the math. Breakfast at McDonalds? You'll need to work about 30 minutes for that. Want your nails done? That's four full hours, please. And add another hour if you want some of Angelah Johnson's *crystal gel* at the nail salon. A new X-Box game? That's 8 or more full hours of laundry, dishes, sweeping, mopping, and yard work, sonny. Concert tickets to that Five Seconds of Fame concert? You'd better give me a full 40-hour week to cover that, missy. Suddenly, I saw their little minds grinding away at numbers before they asked for something new. It's a great exercise in math, and in common sense.

Money management skills should be taught as early as possible. Children should be introduced to and become well aware of budgeting – particularly the problems they may encounter if they go over their budget. The *Gimme Generation* is rarely taught that irresponsible spending leads to real trouble. Your job is to help your children formulate a relevant budget. From their weekly allowance, they should contribute at least something menial towards their entertainment budget. Want to use that smartphone this week? That's ten bucks up front. Want to watch cable TV? The bill is $100 a month, divided by four of us, so that's roughly six dollars a week for your share. Oh, and now you want to go to the movies? Hope you've got another $8.75 lying around, and that's without the six-dollar popcorn and four-dollar soda you can't live without. These seemingly innocuous expenses quickly add up, and making your children aware of and responsible for these invisible expenditures will go a long way in teaching them the value of money.

Step two is to teach them that *saving* is important. There may come that proverbial rainy day when you'll need some extra cash to afford a terrific opportunity or to handle an emergency situation. If you don't have any savings, you might not be able to act responsibly. A wonderful occasion to reinforce this lesson is when something new comes out, like a toy, video game, movie, or something else that your child desperately desires. Pop in your earplugs and don't succumb to begging. Use this as an opportunity to teach them to save enough money to acquire what they really want.

Finally, you need to preach the fact that irresponsible use of credit is evil. It is the indentured servitude of our generation. Most high schoolers graduate without realizing how expensive credit card and loan interest really is. Credit is a wonderfully liberating thing. It allows people of modest means to live like those they envy. Although it's very easy to *sign and drive*, the repayment process can be painful. There is a significant cost associated with borrowing someone else's money over time that can be uncovered in something called amortization schedules. The contractual interest you pay is actually an opportunity cost, potentially disenfranchising you from acquiring something else you may want or need more. When you realize how much interest you're actually paying, it's an enlightening experience that might make you think twice about acquiring a non-essential big ticket item.

The key is getting your children to think about the long term effects of a large-ticket purchase. Smaller purchases can be buried more easily. Although you may be cool with that 60-month $1,200 payment for that shiny new SUV now, I can guarantee you won't be as happy 36 months from now when that ride is dirty, dented, noisy, out-of-warranty, and in need of expensive repairs – and your payment remains at $1,200 a month.

Bad credit can be embarrassing and limiting. You may not be able to purchase the car you want, or to rent a home in a neighborhood with better schools. Many potential employers run credit checks today, and poor credit may prevent you from getting a new job. So much for that right to privacy.

Most schools don't teach students how to balance a checkbook. We opened a checking account and issued our kids ATM cards. Any gifts or allowances are deposited directly into those accounts, and they are responsible for balancing them.

Financial skills are life skills that need to be taught by you in your home, and well before they've made their first million, or more likely, real-world money mistake.

30: the wedding circus

What silly and spoiled New York Yenta made the rule that a bride's family has to pay for the wedding? Maybe that sort of chivalry reigned in the days of regal fiefdom, when only nobility were afforded a true wedding ceremony. Or in the Roaring 1920s at Jay Gatsby's palace, when high-society took pride in showing off how much money they spent. Today, we're talking sequestering, outsourcing, automation, and double digit unemployment. Following those expensive traditions doesn't seem to work as well as it used to. Girls, I hope you've saved your pennies, because your dream wedding is probably on you.

Jake, having spent more than a decade as a wedding DJ, and having lived with a wedding photographer for another ten years, can affirm it is a well-known fact in the wedding vendor circle that weddings are a cash cow business. It is not uncommon for a vendor to increase their prices for the same product or level of service the moment they hear the word *wedding* mentioned in a sentence. Vendors will try to justify their inflated prices using terms like *training* and *backup*, but they won't tell you training and backup are also necessary for any other type of event. Just for fun, we anonymously called a vendor who Jake personally knew on two separate occasions. We asked for prices for exactly the same date, time, and place; once using the dirty word "wedding", and once without. The price was literally *doubled* for the wedding. Try it, and see for yourself.

Paradoxically, wedding vendors rarely incur such expenses. Not because they get better deals, but more so because they too realize weddings have become circuses.

According to The Knot, a website most likely targeted towards first-time brides who are apt to overspend in their wedding expenses, the average wedding expenses averaged about $31,213 in 2014. That is not a misprint, folks. Here are some other statistics from The Knot website from 2013 that may also blow your mind:

- *Most Expensive Place to Get Married: Manhattan, $86,916 average*
- *Least Expensive Place to Get Married: Idaho, $16,159 average*
- *Average Spent on a Wedding Dress: $1,281*
- *Average Marrying Age: Bride, 29; Groom, 31*
- *Average Number of Guests: 138*
- *Most Popular Month to Get Engaged: December (16%)*
- *Average Length of Engagement: 14 months*
- *Most Popular Month to Get Married: June and September (15% each)*
- *Percentage of Destination Weddings: 24%*

Although there are no reliable statistics available pertaining to the average wedding gift, most wedding *experts* (by now, you know how I feel about *experts*) guess newlyweds receive 50 to 75% of their wedding expenditures back in gifts, with a large majority coming from parents and immediate family. I bet it's actually much less. But still, most folks I know don't have that kind of cash laying around for that level of frivolity. Even with a net outlay of $10,000, that's a down payment for a home! Many folks max out their credit cards to facilitate funding the wedding reception. Any respectable financial planner will tell you it's senseless to finance a one-day circus that will provide you with absolutely no utility or little return, especially with 1 in every 2 marriages failing within a few short years. I can't imagine a more painful monthly reminder than paying off a mortgage on a failed marriage.

Traditionally, the bride's family used to pay for:

- *Reception costs, including food, music, decorations, rental fees and entertainment*
- *Ceremony costs including rental fees, decorations*
- *Flowers for ceremony and reception*
- *The bride's wedding dress and accessories*
- *Invitations, announcements, programs, and mailing costs*
- *Favors*
- *Photography*
- *Transportation*
- *Their own attire and travel expenses*

Today, reality has set in. And unless the parents are uppity show offs, today's brides and grooms are now responsible for shouldering most of these costs.

Contrary to popularly accepted social myths and bridal magazines, you can live happily without all the pomp and circumstance that $10,000 an hour will buy you. My wedding was in a windblown ceremony in my back yard. Our trellis blew down, but no one was injured. Our only guests were our children and my father, who took digital photographs that came out perfectly. Net outlay: about $60 in flowers, and a $200 hibachi dinner. At the time of this writing, we've been married 7 years, with no apparent itch as of yet.

DJ Jake had a wedding that had about 100 guests who all had a terrific time. There was a small hotel bar that was rented out for meetings during off-hours, so he got that for a bargain price. "DJ Maxell" (cassette tapes, back in the day) provided the pre-recorded music. Jake's script provided all the traditional breaks, with perfect timing. Jake cleverly MC'd his own reception during those breaks using a wireless microphone. He had a late afternoon wedding that served hors d'oeuvres instead of a full dinner, and Jake paid for the cash bar. These were the days before smartphones, so fortunately, there were a slew of wedding photographers as guests, so they generously took a bunch of photos. Jake's total expenditure? About $3,000. He paid cash. Jake divorced nine years later.

To this day, Jake nor his ex-wife have watched the wedding video or looked at their wedding album.

31: holiday madness

It's not only weddings that have gone insane – birthday and holiday celebrations are silly too. From their origins of celebrating successful harvests, religious occurrences, or historic liberations, today's holidays aren't much more than obligatory gift and greeting card-giving bonanzas driven by marketing companies. Ironically, the word *"holiday"* was derived from *holy day*. I can't think of much that's less holy than today's *holidays*.

Supposedly, sometime during the mid-1600s, The Puritans banned Christmas. Christmas, back in those days, had become a holiday of gluttony and misbehavior and everything that was frowned upon by many Protestants. Puritans believed that Christmas had fallen prey to the traditional and unfortunate European pagan celebrations of the winter solstice, which was symbolized by darkness and underlying evil during the longest night of the year. Think Knecht Ruprecht, Krampus, and the like. If you don't know who that is, you'd better read The Return of Knecht Ruprecht by yours truly.

The Mid-Atlantic States weren't quite as conservative as immigrants continued to ferry pagan customs with them from Europe. The Christmas of Europe was celebrated outside, in the cold and dark, with liquor and spirits and noise and trouble. Eventually, over time, their celebrations calmed down. Well-to-do new Americans migrated indoors for tamer celebrations, with guests slowly becoming limited to close family and friends rather than ill-mannered drunkard strangers. This fostered accountability, which caused much less trouble, and things calmed down for a while.

It wasn't until the mid-1800s that the Christmas blasphemy most Christian people praise and celebrate today began to evolve. If you haven't heard the story, in 1822, Clement Clark-Moore penned a poem entitled *The Night Before Christmas*. His prose was based on St. Nicholas, a fourth-century bishop who was famous for leaving small gifts in cold and damp stockings hung out to dry above fire places. In other stories, there was a separate and unrelated character named "Oden," the pagan god of yule, who, as legend has it, flew through the air on some freakish eight-legged flying horse. Clark-Moore added some fur to the freakish horse, chopped off four of its legs, and decided mere semi-mortal four-legged flying reindeer would be a bit less terrifying. Clark-Moore did a little more mixing and morphing and ultimately introduced his newly invented character, *Santa Claus*. Later, in 1862, a New York illustrator named Thomas Nast read *The Night Before Christmas* and developed the first popularly accepted image of today's Santa Claus. Nast embodied Clark-Moore's St. Nicholas with obesity, ironically foreshadowing a characteristic of more than half of the American population today. Nast also gave birth to the *Naughty and Nice* list, and envisioned Santa living at the pre-global warming still frozen North Pole with enslaved dwarves working in a sweatshop.

Over the past hundred or so years, on the day in which we're supposed to celebrate the birthday of Jesus Christ, the prophesized savior of all humanity, has been further bastardized into a capitalist nightmare. Christmas has metastasized into something far from holy. Ironically, the Christmas season now begins before Halloween.

I'm not conscionably what you'd consider a tree hugger, although perhaps I should be. In the second act of the *Christmas Tragedy*, it is somewhat disturbing that more than thirty million 8 to 10-year-old pine, fir, spruce, balsam, and Frasier trees are slaughtered and sold to families who were told they must have a "Christmas tree" for a proper Christmas celebration. The trees will end up in a landfill, or worse, burned, distributing yet more carbon dioxide into our atmosphere. Supporting the tree tradition eliminates a tree's contribution to reducing our planet's carbon footprint. Fortunately, thanks to your friendly neighborhood fire marshal, most retail stores and businesses are required to display fake trees which are typically reused.

The third act of Christmas involves gluttony. Candy companies have furthered the spread of obesity among adults and children with mass-produced candy canes, gingerbread houses, and the harbinger of all things that are edible but shouldn't be – *fruitcake*. Toy companies ramp up production for their once-a-year festival of plastic production. Electronics and battery manufacturers follow suit. Older, obese, white-haired unshaven men populate red chairs in shopping malls and department stores everywhere, taking small children on their knees and creating false hopes with lies and deceit. There's actually a convention for Santa Claus impersonators called Santa-Con. I found that quite amusing. I hate fights, but I hear there are fistfights between Santas that have got to be priceless to watch.

Soon after October dawns, parents begin to trim expenses and save their hard earned pennies as children everywhere are told to *wait for Christmas*, and their millennial gluttony is placed on a temporary hiatus until December 25th. For on that date, Santa Claus is promised to come and bestow piles of gifts on our children, of which they firmly believe they are entitled to. Parents are guilted into loading their credit cards and they sneak into stores during extended evening holiday shopping hours to purchase thousands of dollars in merchandise that they can't really afford, most of which will be stacked in a closet and forgotten about shortly after the holiday is over.

In some cases, this procedure is a feign display of hope that may buy a day of happiness. Material things have become unfortunate bribery in an effort to apologize for not spending time with children, or to keep up appearances with friends and neighbors.

Christmas Eve is the one day, every year that even the most lackluster Christians find their way to a church pew – some for faith, but largely out of obligation.

Christmas morning arrives. Wide-eyed smiling children filled with hope tear open packages and find the annual supply of Chinese-made products for which they've been waiting for the past several months. Confused American Jewish, Hindu, Buddhist, Islamic, Scientology, and atheist children silently wonder why they too have a Christmas tree.

In many homes, where it's already difficult to make ends meet, many children find disappointment. The expensive electronic gadget everyone is talking about – the one they've seen advertised on television for months – the same apparatus that will make or break their holiday happiness – did not appear in their pile of presents under their tree. After satisfying the promise to *be good* all year, including achieving excellent grades in school and respecting their family and elders, a good-hearted and overachieving child wonders why a neighbor or classmate, who is nowhere near as well behaved or refined, managed to receive that lauded overpriced electronic toy. Dejected parents are forced to formulate even more layers of lies to explain why the promise Santa Claus himself made to them at the shopping mall remains unfulfilled. The irony of how "good" children may feel sad, cheated, and even neglected is painful, at best. But that's no problem, because religious zealots have been trained to quickly invoke that all-encompassing excuse: *God works in mysterious ways.* Whew – tragedy averted.

You can thank several generations of very clever marketing geniuses for setting our society up for a lifetime of depression and the need for chemical additives to stave off such afflictions. *The reason for the season* seems to have been eclipsed. How has such an accountable society and a powerful church allowed this particular ill to perpetrate what is supposed to be a day of joy, celebration and thanks? Perhaps the real question is, how would Jesus Christ Himself feel about what the celebration of his birth has become? It seems we have come to a crossroads of Christianity versus Capitalism. With all the changes happening in Catholicism and Christianity itself, paradoxically, no one has the guts to talk about that. Apparently, it's up to me to begin the conversation.

All men and women should work hard, and they should be justly and fairly rewarded for that hard work. But in our currently entrenched system, humanity worldwide has introduced rewards for dishonesty and greed, where one man knowingly takes advantage of another man's wealth and resources for personal gain. Large organizations have created a deceiving game of psychology called *marketing* that is based on guilt and shame, and firmly endorsed by those society has rewarded the most generously. Following the findings of Sigmund Freud and his nephew Edward Bernays, marketing organizations have been knowingly influencing good children and decent people to believe that this season of gluttony is the norm, through advertisements in every medium they can conceive and commandeer. And we, as parents, have willfully endorsed this behavior without question.

I am not proud that I too have behaved as a lowly sheep, mindlessly succumbing to the whims of corporate magnitude. We have passed a new tradition from generation to generation without ever questioning history, methodology, intent, or accountability. We have allowed, endeared and nurtured a new Puritan nightmare. What was intended to be a fun, heart-warming story, in the mid-1800s, has evolved into a shameful maniacal monster of excess, and I am ashamed. Here is my list of the three things I believe Santa Claus himself needs to do to remedy this silliness.

The word "Christmas" shall no longer be synonymous with plastic or electronic presents, trees, candy, or other frivolousness. If marketers and large companies need a day for gluttony, let us move that celebration to August or September, and celebrate the beginning of a new and successful school year, where children may receive clothing, pencils, supplies, and other useful things.

Christmas shall once again become *Christ Mass*, carefully pronounced that way, in recognition of the holy day it was meant to celebrate. True Christians shall observe mass and celebrate the birth and teachings of the son of their God, Jesus Christ, in a place of worship on Christmas day. Christmas cartoons and movies shall be replaced with Christian teachings of generosity and kindness.

Finally, Saint Nicholas, Kris Kringle, Santa Claus, Knecht Ruprecht, Oden, or any of his other names and likenesses, shall no longer be associated with the Christmas holiday, celebration, imaging, or in any other way, in any country or culture, until the true goodness of Christmas returns.

If Santa were real, I'm sure he would have resigned by now (SPOILER: that's what my Knecht Ruprecht story is about). And if Clarke and Nast were still souls of this Earth, I believe they would revoke Santa's status as the mascot of Christmas.

Now that my Christmas tirade is out of the way, let's discuss the second biggest offender: *birthdays*. Everyone has a birthday, every single year. For billions of years, the earth has travelled around the sun once a year, and for some reason, it has become a worldwide custom to make a big fuss about a person arriving one year closer to his or her death. As a matter of fact, we even celebrate the birthdays of dead people. We have created ghastly traditions of a birthday cake, landfill or ocean-destined balloons, candles, cards, parties, and obligatory gifts. There is even a ridiculous copyrighted song with thoughtless juvenile lyrics of which I may not be permitted to mention without paying a hefty royalty to the descendants of its original author. All this contributes to an already epidemic level of narcissism.

Newsflash: not everyone is happy about becoming another year older.

There's also the Easter bonanza, which has become a mini-Christmas. Children have now learned to expect a Christmas level of spoils accompanied by a one-foot-high hollow chocolate rabbit. And there's Valentine's Day, Grandparent's Day, Secretary's Day, Bacon Day, Corn Chip Day, and literally hundreds of other silly gift-guilting holidays cleverly created by industries looking for a seasonal boost in sales.

As a parent following the rules of society, you'll be forced to participate in this stupidity to avoid painful social chastising. Your only hope is to teach your children the true meaning of holidays, and hope they're strong enough to eventually buck pop culture and make wise decisions on their own. Good luck with that. Your efforts will be tumultuous. Personally, I am embarrassed to admit that I came to this conclusion too late in my life to affect my children. I am attempting to slowly infuse it today. Hopefully, you'll follow this path too. Change has to begin somewhere.

32: family getaways

While walking around a certain well-known Orlando attraction, I noticed an unconscionable amount of mothers with infant children. I wondered why anyone would bring an infant to a place like this. Were they goofy?

Sure, it's cute to see a new mom with her little angel looking all googly-eyed at each other. But honestly, from personal experience, it's a huge waste of time and energy. Mom will be exhausted from pushing the stroller and all the extra baggage, plus she won't be able to ride much, because she's got to watch the rug-rat. Plus, if she's not careful, her child, who hasn't yet developed a strong immune system, may be exposed to a global variety of potentially deadly pathogens. And, who are you really doing this for, Mom? Your child will remember absolutely nothing about this trip as he or she shits his or her pants and smiles.

Mom sits back in her favorite chair as she smiles and looks towards the sky. "Sweety, don't you remember when we went to that park, when you were two?" Her teenaged daughter scratches her head, only half-listening as she giggles and texts her BFF. "Um, nope, not a single memory. Can I have twenty bucks for the movies?"

Hawaii was even worse. On our tour bus in Oahu, I watched a certain bossy new mother who was clever enough to enslave her poor dimwitted Canadian husband with child-rearing duties. He carried all her bags on to the bus, even after an exhausting 12-hour flight with their nine month-old son. Mom smiled as she stared out the window. Her child will completely forget seeing a gorgeous waterfall, the USS Arizona memorial at Pearl Harbor, and the absolute worst shrimp lunch I've ever had. What *we* won't forget is all the loud screaming, getting continually bumped by her stroller, and the permeating smell of baby poop on our tour bus. Thanks for that, eh.

My point is that it's inconvenient and silly to bring any child under the age of 4 on any far-away vacation. Even when they're a little older, you have to really think about the mindset of these kids at the time that you're planning your vacation. Regardless of what you swear you remember from your toddler days, smaller children probably won't be interested and will never remember sightseeing, engineering, nature, art, history, or theatre. If you are into these things and want any hope of enjoying your vacation, you might want to leave your children with someone else, or better yet, reconsider having children in the first place. Some people aren't cut out for the parenting thing. Otherwise, alter your plans to something a little more kid friendly, like Chuck-E-Cheese.

When the kids are a bit older, I'm talking *at least* 8-ish, family vacations are a terrific way to bond, especially in these days of oversaturated electronic communications. Pulling a child out of their element and forcing them to leave their friends, phones, games, and bad habits behind, at least for a moment or two, will give you the opportunity to reconnect with them.

Although I am the most seasick person you could ever meet, we have found the best thing to do is opt for a family cruise.

We refuse to pay extortionate data charges and force our kids to leave their devices behind. Your family will have the opportunity to dine together daily, and you'll share memories of excursions forever. There are affordable cruises that leave from almost every part of the periphery of our country, and some are as short as three days.

If you too are allergic to maritime activities, ask your physician to prescribe a Scop patch. It's a medical miracle. For me, over-the-counter pills and clever bracelets do not work – but this patch thing is crazy good.

Remember, vacation is a time to celebrate life and the gift of family. Try as best you can to leave your nitpicking, nagging, and anger behind, even though your offspring probably deserve it. It becomes extremely awkward when you're miles from home and things get sour between you and your kids. Don't ruin the mood; use the opportunity to patch things up. Vacation time could be the catalyst that makes things better.

33: i-everything

Back in the day, it was easy to keep an eye on your kids. The furthest they might get from your supervision would likely be around the block or at school. In my small neighborhood, there were other equally as astute adults keeping an eye on your kids and keeping them away from trouble.

Today, your children may be physically safer, but they are mentally connected to the entire outside world via the internet. What's worse is that a majority of the influences they are exposed to are largely anonymous. Add on a layer of unsupervised silent privacy, and Dad and Mom may have no idea no the evils your children are viewing. I am still trying to figure out who Slenderman is.

Be aware that it is ridiculously easy for your children to connect with kids from all over the world in game chats and on social media, if you allow it. We're talking different cultures, different political views, different faiths, and potentially other fundamental differences that may not be ethical or even legal in some places. In most cases, conversation with people from other cities, states, and nations is helpful in developing an understanding that there is another world outside of your safe little bubble. But you need to be aware that these outside influences may be out of your control, and in some cases, could be dangerous. Young minds are malleable and easily influenced, so you need to be aware of your child's online friends, conversations, and mindset. You should know their real names, where they're from, and what they're up to. It can be difficult to track the truth, but it's possible. Your best and most effective means to help avoid a negative influence is to only allow usage of these devices while you are in the same room with them, so you can hear at least one side of the conversation – it's always better to hear both. Also helpful in mitigating trouble is to restrict the hours in which your children can use these devices. Seize portable wireless devices before bedtime, and unplug your broadband modem at a certain hour each night if you're concerned.

Kids know that you're trying to watch them. But you're like an enemy spy in a disparaging war. Children believe that you're doing all you can to stop them from having fun. Kids aren't smart enough to understand that you're trying to protect them – and in some cases, the rest of your family. So the dance begins.

Way back in ancient history, like five years ago, MySpace was the dominant social network. They imploded soon after some entitled Harvard kid took over the digital wires. Every kid had a Facebook account, even Peter, until his parents caught wind of Facebook and joined themselves, insisting they became Peter's "friend." Peter was now forced to contain his online behavior. Besides, Peter thought it took too much time to actually type posts and review others on Facebook. What made Facebook even lamer for Peter was that his grandmother joined. She now enjoys exercising her fingers while farming photon crops and crushing candies. Some of Peter's friends migrated to Twitter, where they can keep up with the very important doings of Kim Kardashian and Justin Bieber. If Peter was feeling literal and energetic, he could bitch about anything in 140 characters or less. Some of Peter's other friends swung over to Instagram, where all you have to do is take a perfectly good picture demonstrating what you're up to, and then destroy it with a photo-degrading filter.

Peter liked Instagram because no typing was necessary. Later came Vine. Now, Peter could record a ridiculous short video featuring just about anything, and Peter's equally idiotic friends can see what a freak Peter really is.

Up until that point, you could still monitor your children. But now, with apps like Snapchat, kids can post photos of their private parts and send them directly to their perverted friends. Snapchat deletes the photos seconds after they're viewed so that involved parents, like you, won't have a clue that Peter sent a picture of his peter to Becky. What Peter may not have realized is that Becky was a bit more clever than Peter thought, and she saved a screenshot of Peter's peter and shared it on Reddit, a website where angry, nerdy, and sexually frustrated men hang out.

There are new social networking applications appearing on the scene every day. The game kids play is to use the newest and hottest one before their parents catch on. Fortunately, most kids just watch. But that may be disturbing, too. There is a whole world of unsupervised influence occurring just under your nose. And if you're not aware of those influences, you cannot counteract them or correct any potentially dangerous misconceptions.

Children are children until the day they've packed their stuff up and left your home for the first time. In my little world, while they're still home, they're admitting they are not ready for the real world. So it's your job to continue fulfilling your parenting duties until they've gone. The most important part of your job is providing sound guidance. But it's difficult to provide guidance when you've been shut out. From adolescence forward, a parent's attempt to communicate with children becomes viewed as "nagging" or "stalking."

In today's world, portable electronic devices allow children of all ages to connect with the outside world a little too easily. Think about it this way. Your kid, with his smartphone connected to your unfiltered cellular or WIFI internet connection, now has access to virtually anything in the entire world. He can learn how to ride a bike, play guitar, roll a joint, shoot heroin, or even the proper way for him to give a blow job.

A smartphone in a child's hands is today's equivalent of standing alone, unsupervised, on a street corner in the middle of the night along with a crew of naked, evil, decrepit, and misguided folks. Fortunately, it's usually not a physical meeting, but it has led to that in certain well-publicized situations. It's your job, and not Mark Zuckerberg's, to protect your child from the ills of today's digital society.

When necessary, part of your parental operations center may include CIA-like covert surveillance operations. You may need to know what's really going on in your child's fragile little mind to furtively obtain the correct information you need to counteract anything that might derail his or her education or life. Back in the day, surveillance was easy. You could steam-open a letter and read it, sealing it perfectly before its recipient knew it was read. But the post office is almost out of business. You could stand outside someone's room or pick up another telephone receiver and hear entire conversations. But most folks don't have home phones anymore. Figuring out a password or reviewing computer history was enough information to read confidential emails for a little insight into your child's mind. Kids today consider email as a quaint little antiquity. Texts are not easily trackable. Once they're deleted, it's difficult to un-delete them. Your cell provider keeps all those text messages forever, but good luck getting a subpoena to get your hands on those.

Online video calls via Oovoo, Skype, and iChat are in real time, so they're not recorded. You could overhear those at home, but since the entire technology industry is now going mobile, it's unlikely the kids will make secretive calls at home.

There's only so much you can do to control your child's exposure to the outside world. With that said, there are choices you'll need to make. Should you allow your children to possess or use these communication devices? If you deny them, you risk stifling their technological aptitude, which is now a very relevant skill. If you allow them, you've just invited the entire unfiltered world into your living room.

Most newer routers allow specific filtering, meaning you have the capability to block certain types of internet traffic. Social networking, video chatting, adult subject matter, sex, drugs, and other terms can be filtered, with a bit of complex tweaking of your router. It's not always perfect – things tend to sneak through until the servers they're on are recognized. There is a process called "white-listing," which means you can theoretically list the sites you'll allow certain devices to access on your home network. It's complex, tedious, and will require constant input from you, the network administrator. But that's the ultimate safe-haven for kids.

It's important to realize that cellular devices have the option of bypassing your home network, leaving your router settings irrelevant. Fortunately, some cellular providers also offer some type of filtering or limiting software that can be controlled by the person paying the cellular bill. AT&T offers a service called Smart Limits that runs about five dollars a month, and works very well. Verizon offers something similar.

If you're the type of person who prefers not to apply filters, or if your situation doesn't call for filtering, there are covert ways to infiltrate just about any technology. And to be an effective parent who can provide useful guidance, you're going to need as much information as you can gather. Fortunately, there are now several covert monitoring apps available for both Android and Apple phones. When installed and configured correctly, these apps have the ability to monitor computers and cellular devices and forward most communications, including texts, call logs, social media posts, photos, videos, and web searches from a cellular device. Some of these apps have the ability to block certain applications from running. One has a nifty little feature called "virtual fences." If you've dropped your child off at the mall, this software can be configured to send you an alert if your child has left the mall. It also features GPS tracking, so you'll at least have an idea if your kid is really where he or she said they'd be.

Be aware that some children are quite clever. If Peter said he went to Bobby's house, he could leave his phone in Bobby's mailbox and jet over to Becky's house, or anywhere else for that matter. A GPS monitoring system will still detect the phone at Bobby's house. Most children would die without their phones, so this isn't likely to happen. Until we can legally plant GPS chips in our children, don't think a GPS location app is the solution to the world's problems.

Depending on your personal philosophy, you should be able to restrict access or get enough information for a strong insight into your child's activities using the above methods. But, if you feel you need more, know that most of the commercially available monitoring software will not record telephone conversations. That may be felony in some places, otherwise known as *wiretapping*. A few states do recognize a "vicarious consent" exception, under which a custodial parent may secretly record the conversations of his or her minor child in the interest of protecting the child. Chances are you won't get in any hot water, unless your kid decides to sue you (it happens more often than you'd think). Check with an attorney or your local authorities before you go down this route.

Alternatively, in our home, we instruct our children that we will be watching via *random digital audits*. Since we pay the bills, we feel we have a complete right to check our children's text messages, e-mails, chat logs, phone logs, web history, and social network activities. Children are much less apt to do something wrong or immoral if they think you might be watching to avoid embarrassment, punishment, or a digital curfew. If our kids want to use a digital device, they must agree, in writing, to our rules for a digital audit. Those rules are as follows:

- *You may not delete any text messages or phone logs until we have reviewed them. "Accidental" deletions shall be considered a violation of this policy.*
- *You must supply a verifiable name and relationship for every person we find on your text or phone log.*
- *You must write every social networking user ID and password you use in a log book located in the kitchen drawer within one hour of changing it. In the event we have found outdated information upon a digital audit, you have violated this policy. "I forgot" is not a valid defense.*

- *You must "friend" us or allow us to "follow" you on every social network you subscribe to. You may not ever exclude us from any posts, photos, or any other information.*
- *You may not use a private or cloaked browser, and you may not erase any internet history until we have had the opportunity to review it.*

Children can delete offending text messages and web history, and most social networking sites offer the option to block certain people from seeing certain photos or posts. You need to make it perfectly clear that you will have the means to audit all of their communications. And if you ever find they've deleted something, that's the equivalent of lying. The penalties should be swift and severe, including the surrendering of all digital devices.

Today's millennials either can't spell or are too lazy to type an entire word in texts or internet posts. As a result, *you* have been demoted to *U*. The word "am" has been truncated to the letter *M*. "Are" has been reduced to *R*. "For" is now a number 4, and "to" or "too" is half that at 2. Zeros are randomly used as the letter O, for whatever reasons I can't figure out.

Kids also think they're cool when they pull the proverbial wool over an adult's eyes. But today, it's relatively easy to decipher their codes with nothing more than a Google search. Websites including urbandictionary.com and noslang.com can readily translate even the most obscure text acronyms into plain English. There are hundreds of other shortcuts and code words you should be aware of. Here are a few of the more common terms to catch you up.

- *420 or 4/20 -- marijuana*
- *AWK – awkward*
- *BTW – by the way*
- *CRAY -- crazy*
- *DBA – don't bother asking*
- *DERP -- another name for a weirdo or dork*
- *FML – f*ck my life (indicates depression)*
- *FOMO -- fear of missing out*
- *GNOC – get naked on cam*
- *GTG – got to go*
- *IDK – I don't know*
- *IRL – in real life*
- *KK – okay*
- *L8R – later, as in see you later, or tell you later*
- *LMAO –laughing my ass off*
- *LMFAO –laughing my f-ing ass off*
- *LOL – laughing out loud*
- *MERKED -- being drunk, high, or passed out*
- *MUAH – kiss*
- *NOOB – new person, inexperienced*
- *NP – no problem*
- *OMG – oh my god*
- *POS – parent over shoulder or piece of sh*t*
- *PRON -- porn*
- *PWN – to "own" something, as in being better*
- *ROTF – rolling on the floor (laughing)*
- *SMH – shaking my head*
- *STFU – shut the f*ck up*

- *SWAG/SWAGGER* – *being or having something cool or expensive*
- *TDTM* – *talk dirty to me*
- *TTYL* – *talk to you later*
- *WTF* – *what the f*ck*
- *YOLO* –*you only live once*

And if you're worried about your babies (or their friends) being involved in drugs, be on the lookout for terms like these:

- **Ecstasy** - *molly (molecule) , rolls, stacks, moons, caps, X, beans, skittles, candy, E, MDMA, circles*
- **Marijuana** - *trees, green, kush, dro, zona, hydro*
- **Ketamine** *(an anesthetic used in humans and animals)* - *Special K, Vitamin K, breakfast cereal, K, Ket*
- **Coricidin / DXM (cough syrup)** - *Triple C, CCC, skittles (red pills), tussin, dexing (abusing cough syrup)*
- **Crystal Meth** - *gas, shards, glass, crank, speed, chalk*
- **Heroin** - *antifreeze, dope, brown sugar, horse, tar, train*
- **Cocaine** - *snow, Charlie, dust, lady, snowbird, yahoo*
- **Rig** - *needle used to inject heroin*
- **Crunk** - *to get drunk and high at the same time.*
- **Ritalin** - *pineapple, ritz, kiddie coke, rids*
- **Vaping** - *using a modified e-cigarette*
- **Robotripping** - *using cough syrup*
- **Sizzurp** - *a mixture of Codine syrup, fruit flavored soda, and a Jolly rancher.*

34: general life advice

I couldn't possibly write a chapter on every single parental experience I've had. Plus, if I did that, how could I write a sequel? Momma needs a new pair of Jimmy Choos! But I will leave you and yours with some additional random tidbits and life advice.

There are many things in life that are silly. There is no such thing as ghosts, angels, demons, elves, fairies, or fortune tellers of any type. Don't you think if someone could read the future, they'd constantly win the lottery and buy the world? File this nonsense under "entertainment", and make sure your kids learn to do this too.

Hervé Villechaize was a French actor who looked Mexican yet worked on a tropical island with a superhuman once known as Khan. Hervé has little to nothing to do with parenting, but Villechaize's name on an obscure 1980s television show, Tattoo, has everything to do with some of the worst decisions your sons (and unfortunately daughters) might be making in some dark and dirty backroom right now.

I soon learned that no matter what color you are or where you're from, there weren't many doors that couldn't be opened with a neat haircut, a shave, and a neatly pressed $25 Kohls long-sleeved shirt and tie that covers those wonderfully artistic tattoos. Fake it 'til you make it. Make sure your children are aware that they will be judged by the world, and first impressions are rarely overcome.

A friend of one of our kids barely graduated high school. He was a good looking kid from a well-to-do family. His momma was one of those stay-at-home mothers who spent more time at her wine parties and tennis clubs than at PTA meetings. Basically, her boy ran buck wild, and she didn't care. Boys will be boys, she thought. Her angel decided to take a year off before starting college. That one year became two. Then three. And he's still living with Mom and Dad. You get where this is going. He did manage to find a job at a fast food restaurant. His language began to deteriorate from a non-descript average literate American to something along the lines of a ghetto-dwelling sixth-grade dropout with no front teeph. As he was making money "for the man," he was banking his *fat stacks*, saving for his next round of *ink*. That's right — he was *working for tattoos*.

We chatted one afternoon. Well, he chatted, and I desperately looked through the air below him for subtitles. He was very excited to show off his latest addition to his compilation of tattoos — his new full-color design of some sort of alien-looking plant. Only this time, he chose not to hide it where it could be covered up during a job interview. While he was bragging about how cool he was, all I could think of was how he could possibly get away with wearing a turtleneck at any time of the year in our home state of Florida. I had warned him before that many people weren't quite as open-minded as I was pretending to be, but my warnings fell upon Beats covered ears.

Please, parents, tell your sons and daughters that although tattoos and piercings are fun and trendy and all, most of the non-inked folks sitting behind those hiring desks can be very judgmental. While a single, well-hidden tramp stamp won't hurt anyone in the work world, permanent ink all up in your grill is really a poor decision for most young folks. If you cannot seem to conform to a few silly little rules the rest of society adheres to, how can a hiring manager expect you to be a productive worker who follows their directions? The last thing most people want to hire is a rabble-rouser.

Daddy-daughter dances or Daddy-daughter anything for that matter seems creepy in today's society. Why aren't there *mother-son* dances? My local Chili's sends Jake an e-mail advertising a Daddy and Daughter date night. All participating guests receive a free dessert. Want some candy, little girl? With society assuming every older man with a young girl is a pervert, wouldn't you think they'd opt for a "Family Night" instead?

Speaking of family time… Jake's parents both died young. One of Jake's biggest regrets in life is not having time for his father; he always considered Dad's line of questioning as prying. As Jake got to know his father in his mid-twenties – soon after Jake had hooked up with the wrong girl, had a shotgun wedding and a subsequent daughter – Jake realized his dad was the greatest man in the world. Jake oft wonders how many mistakes he could have avoided had he taken a few moments to talk to his father. And now, as a father with an adolescent son who will soon be too busy for him, Jake further wonders how much joy he stole from his father by blowing him off.

It is so important to be involved in your children's lives as much as possible. But with today's hectic schedule and economics, it can be challenging to find the time. Our rule is dinner time is our family time. The television is shut off, everyone must sit at the kitchen table in an upright position whether they are eating or not, and all phones and portable electronic devices must be turned off and stowed. We go around the table and force everyone to talk about the worst part our days. We then circle around again and talk about the best parts. It was awkward at first, but after a short while, our kids seemed to enjoy it. Typically, I play the "bad cop" by asking silly or leading questions, which usually elicit some kind of response that creates conversation. The kids sometimes hate it, but I try to make it fun. It is a great way to connect.

Looking for more family time? My kids are *really* upset that as a result of the success of our dinner ritual, I have decided that driving time is family time, too. The radio is an excuse for you or your kids not to talk. "Mom, can we play music?" "I would much rather hear about what's going on in your life." Driving in a silent car is quite strange at first, but try it for a while. It's kind of relaxing. Let your inner dialogue work itself out without all that extraneous noise.

And never neg on your kids when they talk to you, or they'll never open up to you again. Find the optimist inside, even if it nearly kills you. Praise them, but be honest. Offer constructive criticism when necessary, and always without being demeaning.

Be your own person. Don't be afraid to have and state your own opinion. It doesn't really matter what your family, friends, or neighbors think about you or how you decide to raise your children. It's none of their business. There are no hard and fast rules for humanity. There is no manual for child rearing, except maybe this one. Step outside the box for a while and you'll learn what really matters in this crazy world that we've created for ourselves. The only thing that will be remembered is that you tried, and gave it all you could.

Take classes with your kids. Learn how to swim, golf, play guitar, ride horses, or mountain bike. Learn CPR. The more you do together, the smarter you'll both become, and the more you'll connect.

Never let any sibling think or know that they are the favorite sibling. This may cause irreparable insecurity, animosity, and other undue negative personality traits for life. No matter how much therapy the lesser sibling receives, he will never get over it. When asked, even if you think you're in a private setting, always answer *"All my children are my favorites."*

Country music is the only music that still has a soul – except for Florida-Georgia line, who are really pop music posers. I mean, really, who raps in country? They're the Nickelback of country! Hip-hop music is an I.Q. numbing recipe for disaster no matter what anyone tells you. Country music songs typically tell a story and many include a positive message, which is much healthier for young and developing synapses. Change all the presets in your minivan to country music stations immediately, and buy Jake McGrew's CD collection.

I saw a meme in my Twitter feed that showed a picture of a mother and child that read something to the effect of "There are only 940 Saturdays from birth and leaving for college." The naysayer in me opened my trusty calculator app and did the math. Eighteen years runs about 936 weeks on the nut, but I'd have to fathom that not everyone goes to college at 18 years and four weeks. Some folks may get 950 to 1,000 Saturdays. Mom had exactly 992 Saturdays with her oldest daughter before she went to college, so take that, meme maker. But that's not really the point.

Some of those Saturdays are going to suck badly. Before you take a deep breath and assume each and every one of those weekends will be a wonderful experience, you should be prepared for Saturdays filled with lip, sass, arguments, sibling fighting, misbehavior, and general malfeasance. Fortunately, that sort of crap usually won't begin until somewhere around your 520th Saturday, assuming you're a wonderful parent, which I know you all are. So to err on the side of an optimist, I'll give you 70% of those 420 Saturdays as good Saturdays.

Now, let's factor in a 50% divorce rate, if you got married at all. You'll now need to split part of those 940 Saturdays with your ex-spouse, whom I'll assume you hate, otherwise he or she wouldn't be your ex. And leading up to your inevitable split, there were probably several Saturdays that you spent being lonely, jealous, depressed, and/or miserable. It's difficult to determine when parents get divorced in the child rearing process, so let's go ahead and assume y'all got a good seven years in before you threw in the towel. And let's conservatively figure that at least 26 of those weeks sucked leading up to the moment you called your attorney. Messy divorces with children can take a year, so factor in another 13 or so weeks of sullen, tear-filled waste. To cap it off, now you've got to split the remaining 576 weeks with someone who will attempt to undermine everything you do for the rest of your child's life.

Unfortunately, many of us send our children to public Petri dish environments known as schools. Your child has probably brought home several unwanted medical maladies the he or she gladly shared with you. Undoubtedly, some of those Saturdays were spent with a box of tissues, a healthy dose of Nyquil, and enough Disney Channel happy-happy puke to make your head explode. Let's shave another, oh, 13 Saturdays off for sickness.

So by my calculations, assuming the above, you may, and that's if you're lucky... I need a spreadsheet. Hang on a second... forget it. Too complex. Public school taught me if it's too complicated, pass it on to someone smarter. Best guess? Conservatively, about 3 out of every 10 of your Saturdays will suck.

The lesson here is that there are no guarantees. God forbid, but there is always the chance your child could be taken from you in an accident, during a crime, or by a health issue long before his or her time. You could meet your own demise prematurely too. Things happen. This is a wonderful world, but it is far from perfect. Remember that life is a finite thing. So do yourself a favor — print this out and pin this on your calendar, right next to that meme. And make sure each and every Saturday counts, good or not.

Always wipe front to back. No one wants poop in their crotch. That makes for a shitty day.

Even if things are terribly wrong, don't forget there are things that might not be so bad. Be thankful for the health and wellness of your children. Things could always be worse. And don't forget to look into their eyes, once in a while, and remember those kids are part of you, and always will be.

And never be too cool to say *I love you*, or to mean it.

about the author

Olivia Black is a pseudonym for an author who is an extremely overqualified parent, an unaffiliated voter, a pistol-packer with a concealed weapons permit, an on-and-off again Philadelphia Eagles fan, and a card-carrying ordained minister of the Universal Life Church of Modesto, California with an honorary but legal PhD in religion.

Black's favorite musical artist is country music's Jake McGrew. Her favorite book, up until this one, was *Falling Forward* by, well, *herself.* It sounds a little pompous, but it's great stuff. Her favorite movie is Contact – it gives her hope for humanity.

Follow Olivia at:
www.livblack.com
www.facebook.com/oliviamblack
twitter.com/RealOliviaBlack

www.ingramcontent.com/pod-product-compliance
Lightning Source LLC
Chambersburg PA
CBHW030423290526
45786CB00001B/113